Social ~~Mis~~ Alignments

The Chiropractor's Guide to Marketing Online

By Stephanie R Beck

Copyright © 2014 SRB Solutions

Forward

I f you are a practicing Chiropractor, you may be asking yourself: Is there a better way to effectively communicate and educate my patients? Are there proven methods to help me get new patients using social media? Can social media save me money and get better results in my office procedures and marketing efforts? The answer is yes, yes and yes.

In this world of ever changing technology, we have learned one thing: people have changed the way they are communicating. Your patients are online looking to make a personal connection with practitioners that care about their wellbeing. For you, social media may not be part of your lifestyle and you may even be unsure of how to take advantage of this popular medium. Changing something as fundamental and deep-seated the way we have traditionally marketed our practices can be intimidating. Yet, for us to move forward, we must acknowledge that the world of communication has changed and learn how to best adapt our message to better connect with our future and current patients. Social Media is one of the quickest ways to make that happen. When we trust experts that understand our profession and how our patients think; we gain knowledge that produces a healthy holistic result for our practices.

In Social MisAlignments, Stephanie provides proven and simple strategies for retaining the patients you have and getting more patients through social media. She doesn't overwhelm you with a bunch of technical information. She explains the concepts, strategies and tactics in ways that allow you to see social media as an opportunity for professional growth. So sit back, relax and be ready to go on a great journey. When you are done, remember that doing it, is the key to success. So let Stephanie guide you and apply what you have learned. This book is the social media adjustment you have been waiting for.

Dr. Fabrizio Mancini
World Renowned Chiropractor, Leader and Educator

Dedication

Dr. Fab Mancini, Dr. Dennis Buckley, Kathryn Feather, Sandra Pearce, Edwena Shock and of course my loving and supportive husband Brian Beck thank you.

Table of Contents:

Chapter 1
Your ~~Social~~ Alignments

W hether you love it, feel it is a waste of time or just do not understand it, the important fact to uncover is what your patients think about social media.

Let me start off by saying social media is not the silver bullet or the "be all end all" to your marketing. It is very powerful and influential, and even a foundational vertebra in the backbone structure of your marketing. You need to have good alignment to operate at a healthy level. Social media can also work like the incredible connective tissue that transmits messages exponentially worldwide or to your local community. There are lots of things social media can do for your practice, but it is just one piece, which when aligned with your other marketing venues, can have amazing results.

The term "Social Media" may conjure up a pain response or produce a grimace much like having a misalignment can cause limited mobility and/or a pain response. As you know, no part of your body escapes the dominance of your nervous system. Improper function of the spine due to misalignments or subluxations can cause poor health or function. Misalignments are also commonly known to reduce the ability of your body to adapt to its ever-changing environment. Even the slightest misalignment of your spine may alter the transmission of nerve impulses, preventing your body from responding properly. Chiropractic is a natural form of health care that uses spinal adjustments to correct these misalignments and restore proper function, helping your body to heal naturally.

Your social marketing plan can have "Social MisAlignments" that may affect other areas of your practice. For example, if your Facebook page, the backbone of most social media, is not set up properly, it can cause your website to function poorly. This can affect your offline contacts with potential patients--booking appointments, visiting your location or making referrals. Social media can affect your chiropractic practice in positive or negative ways.

Subluxations in the body block the right messages from reaching their destination. These subluxations produce painful or negative response through the body. Adjustments correct these subluxations so the right messages produce desired results. The same things can happen with your social misalignments; if they are not connected or not messaging the right information, they can prevent that portion of your practice from responding optimally. The problems might consist of a variety of issues such as less traffic to your website, failing to get new patients, not connecting with current patients in a positive way or not addressing customer service issues. When any of these occur, it produces a painful experience for your chiropractic practice.

The benefit of a chiropractic adjustment is restoring proper function to the nervous system and thus alleviating pain. A patient can experience a significant decrease in pain after just one treatment. Receiving chiropractic adjustments on a regular basis can help the patient to heal naturally and manage pain and stress from chronic physical issues.

Your chiropractic practice may be experiencing poor health in its social media life. It might be experiencing the pain of loss in patient retention and getting patients to make chiropractic care an ongoing priority. Or, perhaps your business needs new patients calling to book appointments. Your social media may not be functioning properly if "traffic" is not getting to your website. In addition, time can be an issue if you are not able to connect and communicate with your patients on a regular basis.

If your social media is not producing the healthy results you expected, perhaps it is time for a social media adjustment! I'm sorry to say that 90% of the social pages I see suffer from what I like to call Social MisAlignments. The message just isn't connecting with the prospects or it is so bland that it has very little relevance for the prospect or the owner is so busy touting how "great they or their practice are" that those posts are like "wallpaper" to the users on the social site. They are overlooked and undervalued. The good news is you can correct it with what I term as making a Social Adjustment. You may need to make several social adjustments but the result is you can create a social site that produces the holistic results you want, need or desire.

Chapter 2
Why Social Adjustments Help

The most common social media sites are Facebook, Google+, Twitter, YouTube, Pinterest and LinkedIn. Social media sites are great tools for doctors who are looking to achieve any or all of the following:

- Increase Brand Awareness
- Develop Customer Relations and Loyalty
- Build Practice Credibility
- Provide Quality Lead Generation
- Increase Conversion Rates for Booking Appointments
- Get Registration for Classes, Seminars, Conferences and Events
- Tractability and Reports for Measuring Results
- Affordable Pay-Per-Click Advertising to Test Market
- Gather Research and Product Development Ideas
- Increase Traffic to Other Sources (such as websites, other social media sites, landing pages, squeeze pages, mobile marketing or blog subscribers.)

Now, some of those terms might seem very foreign to you but don't worry. They were for me, too, when I started studying marketing more than 20 years ago. You do not need to know what each of these terms do. You just need to understand what they do _for_ you in simple language. Remember, people like doing business with people they know, like and trust. That is even more of a factor in the healthcare market. You are already creating these know-like-trust relationships with your patients. So, duplicating those same efforts with your social media should be easier for you than most other types of businesses.

The beauty of today's social media environment is that it gives us some of the best and quickest ways to get people to know, like and trust us. Everything and everybody are online in one form or another. Creating instant connections, making friends and sharing opinions are more global than ever before. Previous to social media sites becoming the rage, communication was limited to health or street fairs, ads on radio or television, or in magazines, journals and newspapers. Introductions from friends, family and patients were the only ways to meet people and develop these know-like-trust relationships. Society today is looking for instant connection now more than ever before. And social media sites are wonderful tools for us, as business owners, to build relationships quickly.

One of the nicest features about social media sites is that you can add just one to your marketing plan and it can remove a social subluxation for you after just a few "treatments." You do not need to try to add more than one at a time unless you have an infrastructure in place to maintain them. Just keep it uncomplicated by adding a Google+ or Facebook page to boost your practice. Once you feel comfortable and get natural health function back to your business, try adding other social media sites such as Twitter, You Tube or Pinterest.

I want to share with you the psychology of the users of social media and provide you with an overview of the different types of social media sites and some strategies to use for your chiropractic practice. You can have a better understanding and appreciation of these sites and determine which one(s) you want to use to remove your "business pain."

Chapter 3
The Psychology in Using Social Media

To appreciate the advantage of social media, let's start by understanding the psychology of why our customers and potential customers are using it. This will have a tremendous effect on how you are going to best use it for growing your practice.

Your goals for your practice, at least from a business or marketing perspective, can be simplified into three words:

- Branding
- Selling
- Promoting

As a business owner, your approach is completely different from your customers when it comes to using social media. Most customers would categorize their time on these sites to one or all of the following:

- Wanting or needing to connect with other people.
- Needing emotional support, validation or recognition.
- Fulfilling their need to have fun or entertainment.
- Using it as a way to put off getting other projects completed.
- A convenient way of getting reviews on products and services from other consumers.
- A way to organize their personal or social life.
- Connecting with friends or family that they may have lost touch with.

By understanding the psychology and motivations of your patients, you can adapt your message to attract your IDEAL patient. Your ideal patient is a person who takes action by engaging with you and yes, purchasing products and services from you. Concentrating on understanding the daily operations and changes of social media only gets you to a certain point.

People who use social media for other non-business-related strategies vary greatly. Some older generations use it to keep in touch with a younger relative that won't communicate any other way. Others are completely the opposite and almost addicted to it. Most of these social addicts spend their lives online and prefer to use social media messaging over email for connecting and communicating.

Which type is your IDEAL patient? Is your customer only using it sparingly or are they the social addict? Do not be fooled into thinking social media is a younger generation's game. My 97-year-old grandmother has been using Facebook to connect with her grandchildren, great grandchildren and her friends for more than a year! If you think about it, what a wonderful way for an aging population to keep connected in life as they start to lose some of their independence. So do not stereotype your audience without doing some research first. You may or may not enjoy using social media sites but the more important thing to know is whether your ideal patient is using them.

Of the list of reasons why customers spend time on social media, three of them will have the most influence on your practice:

- Wanting or needing to connect with other people.
- Needing emotional support, validation or recognition.
- A way to organize their personal or social life.

The key to developing your own unique marketing plan of engagement in your practice will be based on your own understanding of your unique ideal patient.   Let's get started by covering an overview of each of the social media websites, why they are so valuable to your practice and some strategies you can use right from the start.

Chapter 4
Getting Started with Social Media

A lthough social media can be vital to the growth of your chiropractic practice, it is often not a perfect solution. Mostly because this is new technology and we all know technology is always changing. To keep up with the ever-changing wants and needs of the public, each social media site has to continue to evolve. This can prove to be challenging, having to continuously learn and adapt marketing strategies to keep up with the changes. However, despite the learning curve created for people, social media's popularity continues to grow dramatically.

In order to cultivate this new growth for your chiropractic practice with the best results, you will need to have a clearly developed plan. As with any avenue of marketing, you get better results if you have a plan or blueprint for your success. For most business owners, the most painful part of implementing social media comes from using a scattered approach or trying to keep the social media separate from the rest of their marketing plans. To have the best results, you will need to incorporate your social media with the rest of your marketing strategy. This means you must implement a plan to monetize and get leads. One of the best types of planning strategies is to follow the "SMART" goals. SMART goals are: Specific, Measurable, Achievable, Realistic and Time-bound.

Set your goals so you can meet your expectations. What do you want to achieve? Do you want to increase brand awareness? Do you want to have speaking engagements at community events? Do you want to create solid customer retention and longevity? Do you want to build a lead list of potential customers? Do you want people to book appointments? List the things you want to achieve and be sure to prioritize them.

Next, by identifying who your target audience is and knowing the habits of your "ideal" patient, you will be able to connect with them faster. Understand, you can provide chiropractic care to any type of person, but ultimately who is your perfect patient? Whom do you enjoy working with the most?

Also, be sure to include a plan for your content. There is nothing worse than the panic feeling of "what am I going to post today." Craft a theme for each day, week or month. Remember to incorporate any new products, services or events you have scheduled into your promotional content for your social media. There is a later chapter detailing how to create exciting content. So for now, just make a note that you need to plan your content and allot time to measure the results using insight tools and Google Analytics-- both of these will be discussed in the content chapter.

Once you have your plan in place, evaluate the types of social media out there. As mentioned before, the most common sites are Facebook, Google+, Twitter, You Tube, Pinterest and LinkedIn. Now that you have identified your "ideal" patients, spend some time researching where the majority of them are spending their social time. Which of the social media sites are likely to be your best social avenues to connect with them? After you have selected the best place to start, you can then proceed in setting up accounts.

Most social media sites offer personal and business accounts. You might be thinking personal is the way to go since people want to connect with other people. Remember, you are operating a business; therefore, you need to follow the guidelines and recommendations of the site.

In some cases, sites such as Facebook, LinkedIn or Google+, recommend or even require that you first establish a personal account before you can open a business account. You might be thinking, "I barely have time to manage one account; can't I just use my personal account for my business?" My answer to this is **no** because you need to be thinking long term and "big picture." Most business accounts provide benefits and advantages to help you achieve those SMART goals that the personal accounts do not.

Plus, as your practice expands and you start achieving your SMART goals, you may find you need to delegate some responsibilities. Some business sites offer account management features with various parameters, such as:

- Protecting your brand from being hijacked.
- Enabling you to maintain patient confidentiality.
- Being able to separate your business life from your personal life.

Keep your personal account primarily for personal use and your business account primarily for business content.

The reason I say "primarily" is that we have to keep in mind these are "social" sites. People do want to know, like and trust you. So do not be afraid to let your personality show through on your business account. Your friends, fans and followers need to be able to see some of your personal side to connect with you. On the flip side, your personal account doesn't have to be all fun and games. Your chiropractic practice is also a big part of your personal life; it makes sense to share your professional side on your personal account. Next, let's look at some specific strategies for your social media plan.

Stephanie Beck

Chapter 5
Strategies for Social Media

O ne of the best and easiest to implement strategies is one I learned from Amy Porterfield, author of <u>Facebook for Dummies</u>. SRB Solutions uses this strategy for all our customers with great results, so I encourage you to implement it. Use the 80/20 strategy when it comes to content for your social media plan. On your business accounts, keep content 80% informational and educational about your business and 20% personal or promotional. On your personal accounts keep content 80% personal and 20% business or professional.

Here is the simple social media math. If you are posting for your practice on your business page 3 times a day 7 days a week that is 21 posts per week. Applying the 80/20 rule means that approximately 4 posts (21 x 20%) can be promotional.

Other Strategies to Implement:

- You are building a relationship and connecting with your patients and potential patients. This is not a place for constantly promoting chiropractic care.
- Use professional graphics when at all possible. If budgets are limited, at least get a graphic artist to create your timeline header and profile photos for all your social media.
- When someone posts a "like" or shares a "comment," always be sure to acknowledge the post in a timely fashion.

- This isn't a "set it and forget it" plan. You should check your accounts daily if possible. Remember, the main reasons that people use social media are for validation, support and recognition, so reward them for contributing, sharing, commenting and "liking."

- Offer helpful information and links to sites that you think may be beneficial for your customers. Providing the customer with information to assist them also begins to position you as an expert.

Yes, you are an expert! Even if you are a brand new chiropractor, you are already an expert in the eye of your patients. Because, let's face it, **you** took the classes; **you** passed the tests; and **you** know more about chiropractic care than they do.

More Strategies to Consider Implementing:

As you gain momentum, pay attention to why your followers
Invest their time. Are they spending time on the site out of?
Loneliness and isolation?   Do you they love to contribute to a
    cause?
Understanding your ideal target patients' reasons for using social
media will help you to supply the content they find most enjoyable.

Create a feeling of belonging or exclusive membership to your
followers. Because you will capture only a short span of their
time, it is important to be immediately interactive.

Add variety to your content; people love to watch videos and look at photos far more than at text and article links.

Items to Avoid with Social Media:

Letting comments or questions go unanswered for days or weeks at a time. Ignoring your contacts will cause you to lose credibility with your followers.

Losing sight that you are a business person representing your brand.

Straying from the fact that your main follower should be your potential patient.

Sporadically posting.

Bombarding your followers with information and then not posting for days. This inconsistency is not professional.

Using the same format all the time when sharing.

Never checking the tracking tools and options.

Duplicating the same information too often.

Mental Strategy Points

Now that we have covered some of the basics, let's concentrate on getting mentally prepared. One of the first items is to acknowledge that social media specifically gives your "voice" the opportunity to go viral. Concentrate on engaging with key individuals among your desired ideal target audience. Those individuals will always be the ones who are sharing, liking, +1, pinning and tweeting your content and even answering your questions and taking your polls.

If the thought of spending time using social media is painful, it's time to adjust this mindset. Consider your SMART goals and the bigger picture. This is a way to achieve those goals quicker and easier when applied effectively. Think of it as learning a new technique; one that is going to help new patients find you. This does not mean spending hours in front of a computer. In fact, by investing a little of your time in the planning stage, you will be able to spend 30 minutes or less a day to achieve SMART goals. The reason daily attention is important is because of the perceived expectation of people who are using social media sites.

Immediacy is a key component to keeping your audience engaged. Equate it to making a phone call to your friend, asking how they are doing and then hanging up before they answer. That is what it's like when you share information and someone comments, and then you do not respond for 2-3 days. Keep a steady stream of information to avoid constricting your success by posting often and being consistent.

According to an Oracle survey of internet users worldwide, one in six consumers on Facebook expects a response to their questions or

[1]   Oracle "Consumer Views of Live Help Online 2013: A global Perspective, May 14,2012

comments in fewer than 30 minutes. Also interesting, is that more than half of the respondents expect a same-day or sooner response[1]. That is all the more reason to check your social media pages more than once a day.

Be aware of your ideal patients' social media habits. Note items like how often they use social sites. What do you think are the most active days of the week and times of the day for responses to your postings?

Remember, you do not have to answer their question on the spot, for instance, if the posting comes at a time when you are with a patient. It only takes a few seconds to "like", +1 or "re-tweet" their comments from your phone or computer so you can acknowledge them quickly between patients and then respond with more information a little later.

Some practitioners set 5 minutes three times a day to check and respond on their social media sites. If it helps, think of it like checking email or voicemails. You would never go for days or weeks at a time without checking messages on your answering machine or cell phone, so apply that same mindset to your social media sites.

Social media is great to use for lead generation. Use it to drive people to a sales page on your website or to a custom tab within the social media pages. Most social media sites offer special apps to help you connect with your ideal patients.

Be sure to take advantage of these special apps to help your customers find you. For example, Facebook offers check-ins and maps.

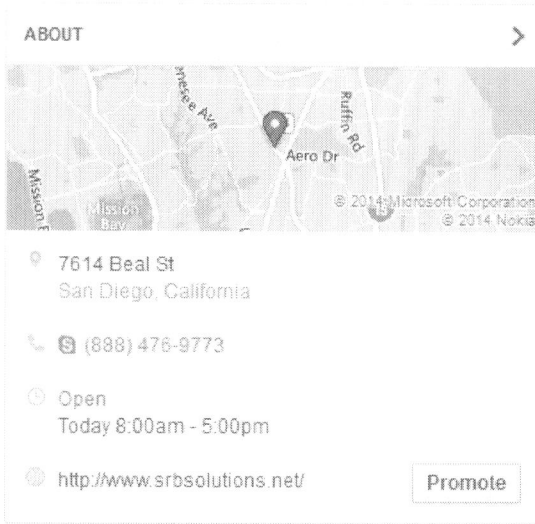

On Google+ you have maps which you can use to direct your customers and potential customers to your physical location.

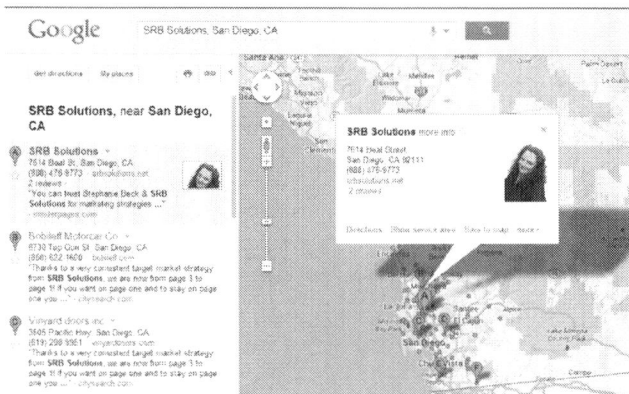

These are just two of the many types of apps available for all your social media sites. A new feature with Pinterest allows you to add a map to your pins. Some apps come standard with photos, videos, notes, likes and events be sure to look for these special features as you start to work with social media sites.

You can also install custom apps. These do require some coding so talk to your website developer or find a programmer to help. Custom apps allow you to connect with your audience and can really boost your lead generating capabilities.

Keep in mind, social media sites are not the ideal tools for direct selling. They work best at generating interest, pushing traffic to sign up for specials offers, creating positive feedback and recommendations, and generating customer loyalty.

Want more strategy ideas? Check out the

www.socialMisAlingments.com/resources page.

Chapter 6
Creating Exciting Content

Remember that first and foremost, these websites are "social." People are there to visit, catch up on events, be educated, have fun and laugh, express their opinions, and share their lives, hopes, dreams, hobbies and interests. One thing they are absolutely NOT using social media sites for is to hear marketing pitches such as: "how-to book on Chiropractic Care," "take my class," "how much patient visit costs" or "buy my products."

The good news is people WILL book your services and buy your products, but only if they are looking to get chiropractic care in the first place or if the information you are providing on your page is interesting to them. So how do you create content that is exciting and interesting?

Start by mapping out a solid content plan. Create a (daily, weekly or monthly) media agenda or calendar. Determine what you are going to post and when, remembering to have a few planned personal shares as well if you are going to use the recommended 80/20 rule.

One of the most frequently asked questions is when and how often to post. Some experts say the weekends are best. Others have said Tuesdays, Fridays and the weekends. The truth is it really depends on your patients' habits. There are some great stats available when it comes to talking about social media as a whole. For example, when evaluating all 1.1 billion users on Facebook, the best recorded days to get "likes" are Tuesday, Thursday and Friday but the best days for commenting and sharing are supposed to be the weekends. Remember, this is taking into account all users and you may find your ideal audience responds differently. When you implement the 80/20 Rule; save the 20% promotional posts for your best times to reach the most people. Review your Google analytics and social media insight tools weekly. Your best days and times will more than likely change. Sometimes these will change weekly. That is why you need to use your analytics and insight tools so you know when the best time to schedule your promotional posts to capture the most people.

Some stats say to post your content before noon while others recommend after 5pm works best. Because your patients will be using social media sites at various times of the day, I recommend using a variety of times with your posts. Schedule one as a morning post between 7am-9am, one between 11am-2pm and one post between 5pm-8pm in the evening. Then use the insight tools and Google Analytics to measure which posts got the best responses.

When evaluating your responses, of course, timing is just one factor. You need to ask yourself, was it the time you posted or the content itself that was so popular? That is why it is best to have the same type of post scheduled at different times of the day and week to identify what works best. So if you schedule an article link Monday morning, try adding an article link Wednesday afternoon or Saturday evening to your schedule. That is not to say to post the same content for a whole week. Using different articles about the same topic are fine, just use different links.

Also keep it fresh--use different types of content. For example, use a variety of ways to post your content including:
- Links to videos.
- Uploaded photos.
- Upload your own videos directly to the social site.
- Links to blog posts.
- Uploaded info graphics.

By using these different methods of sharing your content, you can keep your audience entertained and engaged.

Concentrate on connecting with the ideal patients--they should always become the most active and engaged audience. These are the ones who will share the most, like your posts and answer your questions. You will start to realize their social networking habits, how frequently they are using the site and what time of day works best to connect with them. Until you have established a thorough knowledge of their habits, it will be best to log on three or more times a day.   Just five to 10 minutes will be ample time to review for comments and questions.

Revisit your SMART goals against your content. Is the message you are sharing related to your projected outcome? Is it consistent with your brand message? Have you given your audience an opportunity to join your email list or subscribe to your blog?   How does your theme for the month fit into your SMART goals for your practice? Make a list of key points you want to feature and make sure your social media goals assist with your SMART goals.

Remember that despite the billions of users online each month, they are not there to hear "buy my stuff" messages. The majority are there to chat, get information, be entertained, connect with colleagues, friends and family, give their opinions and share interests. In order for your social media site to work effectively, provide information that interests them but never pushes. They will buy if they are actively searching for your products and services or if the information you provide interests them.

Another recommendation is that you include <u>call to actions</u> (CTAs) with your posts to prompt comments. A call to action is just like it sounds. You are telling the viewer what you want them to do next. They typically are at the very end of your post. The instruction will precede a link of where the person reading the update will go next. Some typical CTAs that I'm sure you have seen are:

- To find out more visit…
- Read more…
- Discover more facts…
- Uncover the real truth…
- Be sure to follow us …
- Click here…
- Register here…
- To enroll…

I used to recommend asking for the "like" or share directly in a post on Facebook. However, due to recent changes, your updates adding these kinds of CTAs to your posts could mean Facebook will actually not show your update in the newsfeed. The types of CTAs NOT to use on Facebook are:

- Click "like"…
- Please Share this …
- Be sure to comment…

Facebook feels these kind of direct CTAs are viewed as spam by their users and your content could potentially be kept from the newsfeed. Some other ways to have a CTA without directly asking for it would be to use the fill-in the blank type of post.

This is a fun way to boost engagement when you create fill-in-the-blank sentences you know your audience will want to comment on. Add in extra twists by including creative images and relating the "fill-in-the-blank" directly to your ideal audience. Another great CTA is to post a photo and ask your customers to create a caption for the photo. Both of these work well for contests so you can reward the best caption or answer. This gets your followers involved and it helps to fulfill three of the psychological reasons people use social media sites: recognition, to have fun and validation.

Use CTAs to gather feedback on products and services. For example, if you are aware of a cool new product, but you want to make sure your patients are interested; ask for their opinion on the benefits. This type of feedback can be extremely valuable and can create some intrigue and excitement around new retail products.

The main strategy when it comes to creating great content is to know your audience and understand what makes them tick. Once you know what topics, words and emotions trigger them to take action, and then it becomes much easier to craft the perfect posts that demand engagement.

When you start sharing content, do not get discouraged if you get an occasional complaint. The best thing to do is respond promptly. Some doctors want to delete the post. I offer another scenario: let's say you have a complaint that has been posted for two hours. You weren't aware of it because you were taking care of patients and didn't have time to check the posts. How do you deal with it?

Instead of getting angry and deleting the post or reacting negatively, post your solution to the problem or offer to communicate to a solution source. I have seen instances where loyal customers defended a business when another person posted negative comments, even before the owner had a chance to respond. Your patients and followers will grow to admire, respect and like you the more you build the relationship.

A great benefit to creating exciting content is it attracts more people to "like, comment, follow, re-tweet, +1, subscribe, and re-pin" your content. The more they follow your practice, the more likely they are to read what others are saying about your practice.

So far, you have learned why social media sites can help you, the psychology of using them, and an overview of strategies and content. Now, let's get a little more specific about each of the TOP 6 Social Media Sites: **Facebook, Google+, Twitter, YouTube, Pinterest, and LinkedIn.** More than likely, you will begin with either Facebook or Google+. The reason I consider Facebook and Google+ to be more important social media sites is logical. I choose Facebook due to the sheer number of users and popularity and

Google+ simply because of Search Engine Optimization and recent rapid popularity growth.

The third most important site to review is Twitter because their fans are very loyal and seem to be raving followers. I like Twitter because it has such a fast moving pace and connects so well to all the rest of the social media sites.

YouTube (which is owned by Google) is considered by some to be the second largest search engine and can boost your social media if you implement the right strategy.

Pinterest is one of the newest social media sites and is very visual; much like YouTube, if implemented with the right strategy; it can be a powerful asset for your practice. In fact, based on 2014 placed pins, experts are saying Pinterest could be giving Google a run for their money as a top search engine over the next year. LinkedIn also has many advantages and can be used in a variety of plans for the growth of your practice.

As you can imagine, each of these social media sites could have their own individual book. Not to overwhelm you with a bunch of information, these next six chapters are meant to provide you with general overviews, real strategies and action steps. The real strategies and action steps are meant to be more "big picture" than step-by-step details. By providing "big picture" information with a broader view, ideally the strategies and action steps should be ones you can apply immediately to get you started or to update what you already have in place.

If you would like more in-depth step-by-step training on how to set and use social media be sure to visit: www.socialMisAlignment.com

Stephanie Beck

Chapter 7
Facebook: Fresh Start or Freshen Up Your Look

Facebook is one of the most popular sites around the globe. Unlike other social media websites that have lost popularity, it is pretty likely to be here for the long run. To date, Facebook has more than one billion users and those numbers are expanding daily. So, let's walk through the basic steps of creating a business account and include advanced notes for those of you who already have accounts but may need to update your strategy.

Facebook guidelines strongly recommend against using personal accounts for business. They encourage businesses to have business pages by offering special features that personal profiles do not have.

Some doctors make it a policy not to accept "friend" requests from patients because they want to maintain professional boundaries. Therefore, a business fan page is the perfect way to connect with patients and keep family and acquaintances for "friend" requests.

Sometimes, it isn't that simple. When I first started using Facebook, I was employed by a company, so I created my brand using my name and personal account. My close friends and family understood that the majority of my "friends" were actually patients and the bulk of my posts were business related.

How to Know the difference Between a Personal Page and a Business Page.

Lots of practitioners have asked, "How do I know if I have set up a personal page or a business page?" You can tell the difference between them by looking at their headers (the big photo at the top of the account). I've included two examples – the first is my personal account. You can tell it is a personal page because it offers a way to make "Friends." On the Business page, someone can only "Like" the page or become "Fans" of the page.

Once I launched SRB Solutions, I set up a business page and I still maintain both accounts. However, trying to get customer "friends" to switch over to my business page rather than my personal profile has been a little challenging. Therefore, I recommend you save yourself this hassle and use a business account from the start.

If your goal is to use Facebook to build your business, in the long run, I recommend you establish a business page. You can create a business page from pretty much anywhere on Facebook. Look for the words "create a page" on buttons or at the bottom of your profile account. When you are setting up your page, one of the first items you will notice is that you have six types of pages to choose from:

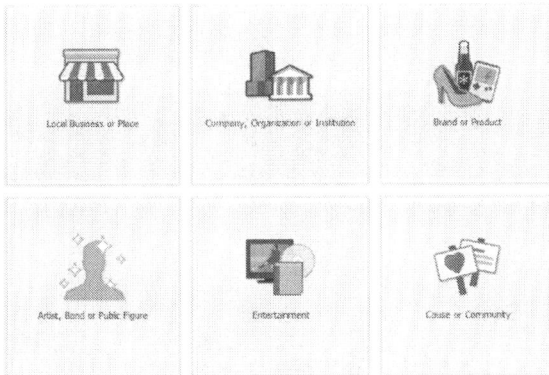

This isn't a permanent decision and can be changed even after you "go live" should you decide or need to change it later. For example, you may start out working from home, so you choose "Company, organization or institution," but after a couple of years you start renting office space. You can change your type to "local business or place." Each category has different features and benefits associated with it. For example, the Local Business or Place allows you to pull in map locations for customers to find you.

Advanced Note: If your company/brand name does not include a keyword when creating a name of your page, include your brand name and one keyword for Search Engine Optimization (SEO) ranking purposes.

Next, you want to complete every part of the "about" section and use those keywords (special words that your patients and potential patients would type in to find help) as naturally as possible into the about sections. Add links to your website. Because this is so important, I'm going to say it again, be sure to complete every portion. All of those items should assist you with your SEO ranking.

Advanced Note: Include a CTA or offer with a live link in the first 27 characters of your short description that shows directly on your page. If you are a local business, your website, phone, address, hours and name will appear in this area so be sure you have everything completed.

After creating your business page, you should start getting as many people as you can to view and "like" your page and you want it to happen fairly quickly.

Remember, your goal is have your targeted ideal patients liking your page. These are the ones who are most likely to do business with you. Plus, you want people who will actually be active and engaged on your Facebook page.

There are some advantages to getting your first 30 "likes." This will unlock your <u>insight tool</u> for your page and allow you to establish a <u>custom URL</u>.

Your **insight tool** is valuable because it allows you to know how you are connecting to your customers. The insight tool tells you what your customer like best about your posts and what day and times your fans are on Facebook. It can be found on your admin panel above your timeline header and is only seen by administrators of the page.

A **custom URL**, also known as a vanity URL, is a shortened website link directly to your page. When you first set up your page, the URL has the name of Facebook, your page and then a series of numbers that might look something like this: http://www.facebook.com/srbsolutions_10203938580973279823.

When you have reached more than 30 "likes," you can set up a custom/vanity URL. In the admin panel on Facebook, they refer to it as your user name, which will be something like this: http://www.facebook.com/srbsolutions

Advanced Note: Your custom/vanity user name can be a keyword for SEO purposes and does not have to be the same as the page name. For example, if you were a chiropractor in San Diego, the name of your business might be "Smith Chiropractic" but you could make the custom URL of your page www.facebook.com/ChiropractorSanDiego

Once you have your custom URL, be sure to use that link on all your other social media websites and add your Facebook buttons on those websites. Include your page link on your emails and add the social icon to any direct marketing piece such as your business cards, advertising, flyers, postcards, etc.

Some people feel they want to have a custom URL before inviting all their friends, patients and family to visit their page. I feel like it is more important to start taking action right away by inviting your patients, friends and family members to like the page, especially those who have a lot of friends.

The reason you want to make fans with people who already have a lot of friends is their friends will see the notification when they have "liked" your page and some of them will visit your page just because their friends or family "liked" your page. This is called social reach and is important for getting your posts to go "viral."

 If you do not have an existing patient list or feel awkward about asking your friends and relatives to "like" your page, you might consider running a like campaign to drive traffic to your page. This doesn't have to a high cost and generally you can get a nice boost to your likes within the $20-$50 range.

Another way would be to find community pages or groups where your ideal targeted audience is investing their time and "like" the page as your business page. Instead of liking another business page as yourself (personal profile) you have an option to like a page as a page you manage. For example, when potential business customers send me personal requests to "like" their page, instead of Stephanie Beck liking them, I have SRB Solutions like them. It is simple to do. Find a page that really matches up with the targeted audience for your practice. Before you click the "like" button, select the drop down arrow next to the gear icon. You should see "like as your page…" as an option. Select this option.

Advanced Note: If you have multiple business pages connected to your personal profile after you select this option, a second window will appear and you will need to select which page you want to like this as.

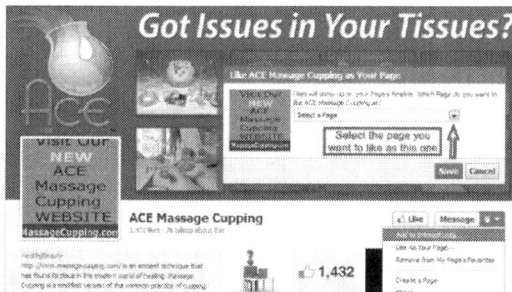

You will also want to visit these community pages frequently. Comment and share these community pages as your page, especially the ones that have multiple fans who could be your ideal patients. In order to make comments on the other page as your practice instead of you personally, you will need to change your "voice." You do this by selecting the gear icon in the upper right-hand corner of the page. From the drop down menu, it will give you an option to "Use Facebook as:" and you select from the pages you manage when you want to post, comment and like on Facebook.

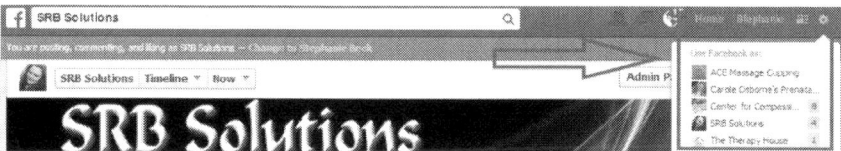

After you have finished making comments as your page, you can switch your voice back by selecting the gear icon and this time select use Facebook as Your Name, and now you will be posting, commenting and liking as yourself.

Facebook Featuring Content

When you start posting content, you will want to feature the most important posts; in other words, the ones your ideal patients will find most important. You can feature the post by pinning it to the top of the page. Be sure to invite your friends and customers to your new page and ask them to check it out.

Advanced Note: Work keywords (SEO) within the first 18 characters of a status update to serve as the SEO title.

You can pin, highlight or feature different status updates. When you pin a post, it will stay at the top of your page, so it is the first post anyone coming to your page will see for the next seven days or until you take it down. After seven days, the post will be replaced back in order by date of posts on your page. You can change pins and re-pin any post from your page at any time but you can only have one pin per page.

When you are considering what to highlight and pin, be aware of the number of shares and comments your content is getting. A good strategy is to allow a post to mature for 20-30 minutes before deciding to highlight or pin. Pay attention to the number of "shares" and "comments." This is a great way to learn what really triggers and engages your audience. It also lets you know which subjects or topics are ignored.   Review all your stats for multiple posts by revisiting your insights tool at least once a week.

The reason you want more shares and comments is because all engagement of your Facebook page is measured by a complex algorithm. This Facebook algorithm is used to identify the popularity of pages and how high your updates will be in your fan's news feeds. When your fans like, share and comment on all your posts frequently, your Facebook page gets a higher score and is considered more valuable to your fans and, therefore, when your fans log in, Facebook will make sure your posts are higher on their news feed.

This is why it is so important to be consistent with your posts and respond to your fans in a timely manner when they comment or share posts. If you do not post frequently or consistently, your score will fall and you will not be as high on your fans news feed.

Typically, only about 3% to 4% of your fans actually see your posts. This number can be higher or lower depending on the frequency and type of content you are posting. If they are not engaged on your page, your posts will be lower in the news feed when they log on. The average Facebook user spends approximately twenty minutes on Facebook daily. If your fans only have 20 minutes, more than likely they are only going to respond, (like, share and comment) to the posts that are at the top of their news feeds. Simply put, having fans "like" your page does not insure they are seeing every post.

Just as important is that you are consistently providing updates to your page. If you only post three days a week and your fans are logging on every day, you will lose credibility because there is nothing new for them to see, like, comment or share. Therefore, you could drop position in their news feed.

A better strategy is to post daily with a variety of information in various formats. That way, even if your audience only logs in three days a week, there are more times for your fans to like, share and comment on the variety of topics. Your fans must be engaged with the content you are posting to have the most success.

Some doctors are concerned about "over posting." This is where the value of your content needs to be watched. Go back and review the Creating Exciting Content chapter and implement those strategies so you can position your social media site to have the best chance at achieving your SMART goals.

Advanced Note: Photos, videos and other interactive app-based posts are watched more prominently by Facebook.

10 Action Steps for Facebook:

1. Be sure you create a business page for your chiropractic practice.
2. Feature Keywords (SEO) in your page name and custom/vanity URL.
3. Complete all information on your page and include keywords (SEO).
4. Communicate and like community pages as your business page.

5. Create and build relationships with your fans regularly (daily). Commit to spending 10 minutes a day signed in on your Facebook page.

6. Feature and highlight posts using a variety of media such as videos, photos, article links, blog links and links to custom apps.

7. Make full use of all apps, surveys and cross link to other social networks and your website.

8. Do not think about sales or dollars when you are sharing content.

9. Encourage your patients to write recommendations and visit your page.

10. Share content from other pages on your page.

With more than one billion users and over 500 million logged in every day, Facebook can be an efficient, powerful social media website to growing your chiropractic practice when it is used effectively.

Please connect with me on Facebook- visit our www.SocialMisAlignments/profiles you will find my Facebook Page link – I look forward to liking, sharing and commenting with you soon!

Stephanie Beck

Chapter 8
Promoting Your Practice with Google+

About a year ago, Google+ Local replaced Google Places and it appears still to this day that Google+ seems to be in a constant state of change. This is met with a lot less frustration, swearing and crying than a few years ago because most everyone seems to be adapting to the constant state of flux happening in other online marketing. As a whole, we are learning to be quite flexible and good at struggling through learning the "new systems" when the changes happen.

With more than a billion people searching on Google every day, Google+ Business Page attracts new customers and builds deeper relationships with current customers. To date, there are more than 170 million people using Google+ to connect both personally and professionally and that number continues to rapidly expand daily.

To get your practice on Google+, you will have to first create a Google+ profile. Just like with Facebook, Google+ profiles act as the owner of the business page. Even if you already have a Google+ page, continue reading through and pay attention to the advanced notes and strategies you can apply to your existing account.

A special benefit that makes Google+ so user friendly for business owners is that you can add additional managers to your page to assist you with your marketing.

Special Note: When you are setting up your personal profile, Google recommends you use your real name and not a business name or your account could be suspended!

You can also access your Google+ account by logging into your Gmail and look for your name+ in the upper left corner of the page. If you click that, you will see your Google+ personal profile.

Once there, if you hover over the home, a drop down screen will open up and you can click on pages from that screen.

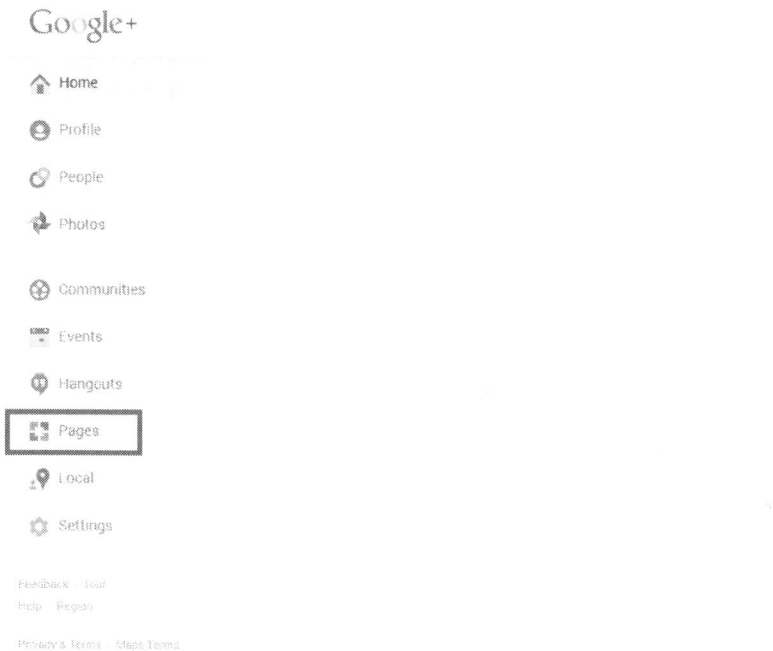

Google+

- Home
- Profile
- People
- Photos

- Communities
- Events
- Hangouts
- Pages
- Local
- Settings

Feedback   Tour
Help   Region
Privacy & Terms   More from

One of the first items you will need to do is select a category on the left that best describes the type of page you want to create.   You will notice these are very similar to ones in Facebook.

When you pick a category, additional drop down fields will open. Select the most appropriate for your practice. Enter your page name and website if you have one, agree to the page terms and click "continue." Be sure to add professional graphics to your photo, your photo size is 2120 x 1192 pixels in size. Leave a 25 pixel margin on either side of official Google Graphics and other text or graphics on your page. Complete all the sections including your "about" sections and add in photos and videos so you have plenty of content.

Advanced Note: Be sure to include Keywords (SEO) and CTA in your story and about sections.

You are going to want to promote your page in all areas of marketing both online (website, email, other social media sites) and offline (in your clinic, on flyers, business cards, invoices, postcards, ads, etc.)

Also follow other Google+ pages to discover where your ideal customers are spending their time. Be sure to engage with these pages, re-sharing and commenting on their posts.

Advanced Note: If you use Adwords, pay attention to this essential step. Turn on social extensions, which show a 5-10% increase in click-through rate (CTR).

Follow your SMART goals and marketing plan for your content (this will be similar to your Facebook plan covered earlier).

Review the Creating Exciting Content chapter to ensure you are delivering valuable content to your circles.

The one new advantage to Google+ is <u>Google Hangouts</u>. If you haven't tried this new feature yet, do not wait any longer. These multi-person video chats allow you to interview patients or get customer feedback; you can make announcements about new services or products and demonstrate the benefits of new a therapy or retail products. Or, show off new additions to your office or waiting rooms and much more.

This may sound a lot like videos, the biggest difference is your editing and rendering time is reduced and Google indexes almost immediately which means no more waiting for videos on YouTube to rank! So, you do need to spend a little extra time in planning. Consider who you want participating, make sure you have good lighting and keep your talking points handy. Encourage the conversation if there is a lull. It also will be good to practice before hand.

So, why should you consider using a Google Plus local page for your practice? Below are five reasons to consider using Google+ Local Pages.

1. Social Media and Google experts are certain that as Google continues to expand their products and services, it will

surely become as powerful of a social media site as Facebook.

2. Next to a paid ad, Google+ Local Business pages are starting to achieve top, first page ranking of local organic Google searches.

3. Because Google owns Google+ pages, content posted on pages is indexed for SEO ranking purposes quicker and some say easier than with other social media websites.

4. Easy to use Google Hangouts gives more of a personal conversation with your patients and followers.

5. The easy use of the +1 Button. When customers and potential customers are logged into Google, they see if others have "recommended" your practice. And if they have already liked your business, they can press the +1 button for themselves to recommend your business to others.

Advanced Note: Google+1 button can be powerful! Add the +1 button to your blog. Create a (CTA) call to action to "recommend" your practice and add the Google+ icon on your website, blog and email.

The power of the +1 button for your online marketing is for business pages only and will not work for profiles.

A big difference between Google+ profiles and business pages is the privacy settings. You can choose and customize privacy levels with your personal profile, but business pages are always public.

9 Action Steps for Setting Up a Google+ Business Page

1. Be sure you create a business Google+ page for your practice.
2. Complete all information on your page and include keywords (SEO).
3. Create a marketing map and agenda for your content to share.
4. Engage, re-share and comment on other Google+ pages where your ideal patients are spending time.
5. Create and build relationships with people in your circles by regularly committing to spend 10 minutes a day.
6. Install the Google+ button on all online and offline marketing.
7. Use Google Hangouts for interacting with patients, sharing new services and connecting with people in your circles.
8. Follow content strategies and measure against your SMART goals.
9. Encourage your patients to +1 recommend and leave reviews on your page.

With more than a billion people searching on Google daily, hopefully it is easy to see why Google+ Business pages can be a powerful social media website for your practice. Utilize keywords (SEO) in your content on your Google+ Business pages and Hangouts to connect, share and rank your practice so new patients can easily find you.

Please follow our Google+ Page so I can follow yours. If you share me in your circles, I will be sure to add you to mine- the links are on www.socialMisAlignments.com/profiles .

Stephanie Beck

Chapter 9
Why Twitter Can Be Great for Your Practice

To date, there are more than 400 million Tweets a day and 200 million active users. It is fair to say people turn to Twitter to draw them closer to things they care about. So, is it necessary to have a Twitter account? If you already have a Facebook and Google+ business page, why would you want to set up a Twitter account?

Generally speaking, everyone has their favorite social media website. You won't find a lot of people who spend their time on all social media sites. Most people who spend their time on Facebook will not be big Twitter users and vice versa. So, the beauty of using Twitter is it can open a whole new pool of potential customers. Even if you are not a fan of Twitter, you should find out if your ideal patients are spending time on Twitter. If your ideal patients are using Twitter, then like it or not, you should consider setting up an account.

Understanding Why People Use Twitter

Twitter was founded in 2006, and started out as a text message service that enabled users to quickly communicate with a small group. Since that time, it has evolved into a global service. An important difference between Twitter and other social websites is that everything you post on Twitter is **Public**.

Think of Twitter as short bursts of information because every message is limited to 140 characters, otherwise known as "tweets."

Even though you can access Twitter from desktops, laptops and tablets, more than 60% of tweets are from mobile devices.

Millions of people use Twitter to discuss everything from news to brands and business. Yes, EVERYTHING. From chiropractic CE's to treatments to research to course requirements to back pain to remedies. Everything is being discussed on Twitter daily.

People are using Twitter for the exact same reasons we previously listed, they simply prefer this method of communication. Yet, a lot of the same guidelines and rules apply to using this social media as with the others discussed.

Getting Started or Updating Your Twitter Account

Just as with Facebook and Google+, you have a profile photo and banner. Below are some important tips:

Keep your "handle" as short as possible. The longer it is the less characters people will have when replying to your tweets.

Your handle can also be a keyword (SEO). You may want to include your best keyword in your handle, if you want to be found that way.

Your handle can be changed at any time, pending availability. Most spam handles have numbers in them, therefore, to create a spam-free handle, avoid including sets of numbers in your handle (e.g. @name456789)

Be sure to include a CTA in your header. Create a custom CTA because you can change this often to promote several different CTAs.

Just like with other social media sites, you will want to complete the bio and invite your patients to follow you.

Advanced Note: Include the main keyword (SEO) in your bio that accurately reflects your chiropractic practice. You only have 160 characters so make it count.

Search engines often display your Twitter bio in the link descriptions on the results pages so make sure you use an attention grabbing statement.

Once the background and profile is complete, begin to search for your ideal audience and follow them. One way to get followers is to follow them and follow other brands they follow.

How Do You Find and Get Followers?

You need to create some sweet "tweets." Content, content, content is a key player on all social websites. Twitter is a little different because you are limited in the number of characters. Between 120-130 characters seems to have the highest click through rates (CTR). Craft your tweets in advance and measure them against your SMART goals. Twitter is fast bursts of short bits of information. Due to this quick pace, plan on twice as many updates (daily) than with other social media sites. Otherwise, your tweets will surely be swept away in the rush of other tweets.

Search engines like Google and Bing have shared that the value of Twitter authority correlates with the value of the link posted. Search engines are analyzing the number of times your content is re-tweeted in order to give the re-tweeted link its proper value of importance. This is the Twitter equivalent of an inbound link. If that seemed confusing, here is a simple way of explaining it: posting updates that appeal to influencers will inevitably boost your optimization efforts.

How Do Hashtags Work?

Hashtags are useful for attracting the right followers and finding the right people to follow and hooking into the best network segment for your SMART goals. Hashtags can be a keyword (SEO), hook (offer), topic indicator, community connection and a search filter all in one!

You can sort through the spamming tweets by searching the keyword (hashtag) in your filter. It also makes it easy for your audience to find you when you share your hashtag.

Hashtags can be a word, acronym or collection of characters proceeded by this symbol #. Some examples are #Chiropractic Care, #backpain.

You can create your own, follow other peoples' or follow a company or resource hashtag.

Google+, Pinterest, YouTube, and most recently, Facebook also allow hashtags, although Pinterest hashtags are not the same as Twitter so make sure you study each social media's specific guidelines before you start.

Benefits of Using Hashtags

- Multiply your following.
- Find your ideal target audience.
- Brand your practice i.e. #SRBSolutions.
- Participate in Tweet Chats and Twitter Parties.
- Tweet information quickly.
- Network with others in the chiropractic profession.
- Increase traffic to websites, other social media sites, clinic, events and more.

If you are going to use hashtags, remember to save them for the important and highly relevant information. If you get lucky, they could go viral! Make sure they are short, catchy and easy to read by selecting the right keyword(s) that your ideal patients would find most interesting. Another strategy is to pair your new hashtag with another relevant active hashtag.

Of course, the more followers you have the more likely your hashtag is to be re-tweeted and followed. Following the right people can also help boost your own credibility, just make sure the people are consistent with your brand and stated core values.

You can also dilute the effectiveness of hashtags if you overload your tweets with too many hashtags or add hashtags that are non-related to your topic.

Implore the KISS method – keep it super simple when using hashtags. Focus on your goal and your followers. Make it easy to read, remember and re-tweet.

Why Retweets are Important to Your Practice

Re-tweeting is considered to be the most over-used and least understood feature of Twitter. But re-tweeting can help you grow your traffic like no other strategy!

Basically, re-tweeting means you are sharing someone else's tweet with your followers. By doing this, you are endorsing and recommending this person or company.

Getting your information re-tweeted by an industry influencer that your target audience follows can boost your credibility almost immediately.

Advanced Note: To manually retweet, open up a new tweet type RT, plus the Twitter handle copy and paste the tweet text. Paste it after the RT@handlename.

Re-tweeting Tips:

- Write tweets that are short so others can manually customize and re-tweet. The most popular re-tweets is 71-100 characters.

- Mix re-tweets in with other tweets.
- Use re-tweets sparingly and strategically – you don't want to be labeled as a "re-tweeter."
- Ask for re-tweets.
- Find who has re-tweeted your posts by selecting "Notifications" and reviewing interactions and mentions.

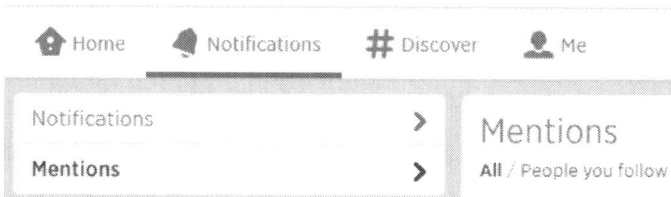

🏠 Home	🔔 Notifications	# Discover	👤 Me

Notifications	>	Mentions
Mentions	>	All / People you follow

Some Quick Etiquette Tips for Twitter:

To tweet or not to Tweet; that is the question. Only reply when necessary – a polite thank you is not valued – save the replies for ongoing questions and comments.

Follow your followers to allow direct messaging (DM) - you can only direct message your followers when you follow them back. DM can be a really powerful tool for answering questions and handling customer service issues privately, so make the time to always follow back your followers.

Placement of the @ differentiates between a "reply" and a "mention" – placing a @handle name in front of a tweet registers as a reply by Twitter. Placing it anywhere else, Twitter considers that to be a mention. When you reply, that only shows up on your profile page and the feeds of people who follow you both.

Pre-plan your tweets – have them pre-written and ready to go to minimize your daily activities.

Frequently check status- things move fast on Twitter and you want to be able to respond and comment quickly.

Keep tweets conversational.

Use your humor – make it fun but keep it professional.

Add photos with tweets whenever possible.

Make it shareable –create funny, helpful, newsworthy or inspiring tweets.

Ask questions – ask for opinions, feedback, use it for research.

Use for special events and social occasions.

Tweets containing links are shared more often than those without.

Don't become a serial re-tweeter!

Use URL shorteners to give your followers more characters to customize.

Studies have confirmed using the word "please" in your tweets gets re-tweeted more often.

How Often to Tweet?

This is where Twitter really differentiates itself from other social websites. Believe it or not, 15 to 25 tweets per day are considered the "sweet spot" for increasing followers. If that number freaks you out, remember that is an average and you can adjust the number you want to use. I found as little as 2 to 3 tweets per day will result in a steady flow of followers. What is important is that too much posting, posting the wrong information and posting too often, can decrease your opportunities to grow and reach. This is why content is so important.

10 Action Steps for Twitter

1. Create a short, catchy handle.
2. Complete all the profile information and use keywords (SEO).
3. Use professional graphics with CTA's.
4. Create a marketing map and agenda of your content using your SMART goals.
5. Tweet frequently and daily 2 to 25 times a day (depending on your audience).
6. Follow your followers so you can send direct messages.
7. Create and save hashtags for special occasions.
8. Use re-tweets sparingly and strategically.
9. Add your Twitter and Hashtags (when appropriate) to your online and offline marketing.

10. Be polite, use links, ay please and ask for re-tweets.

More than 32 billion people search daily on Twitter for topics, reviews, comments, events and other helpful information.   That is why using these action steps, strategies and tips are vital to making Twitter a social media site for your chiropractic practice.

Be sure to follow me, I will follow you back @SRBSolutions.

Stephanie Beck

Chapter 10
YouTube: Vital for Your Practice

B y now you are posting, +1ing and tweeting like a pro. You have your content marketing plan and are set up to achieve your SMART goals. But have you set up your YouTube channel yet?

Before you decide that YouTube is not your "thing," keep in mind, it has more than one billion users visiting each month. YouTube's own stats boast more than six billion hours of video are watched each month! That's almost an hour for every person on Earth! According to Nielsen, YouTube reaches more U.S. adults ages 18 to34 than any cable network. Do you have any customers in that age bracket? Did you know more than 25% of all YouTube viewing is through mobile devices? Customers are watching more than funny cat and blooper videos! Patients and customers are watching "how to" videos, reviews and testimonials about products. Why shouldn't they be watching your videos?

YouTube Benefits for Your Practice

The reason video is such a powerful social networking tool for your practice is because it provides a personal contact and immediacy as no other medium does. Remember the benefits of Google Hangouts? The list included interviewing patients, gathering customer feedback, making announcements about new services or products, demonstrating the benefits of new therapy or products for patients, and more. The same benefits apply with your YouTube channel.

Because Google owns YouTube, all videos are indexed quicker for SEO ranking purposes than if you use other sources. The trick is, of course, to know what your Ideal patients want to watch. As you can imagine, there are specific strategies to make YouTube a social media site that will work for your practice. Plus, you need to create your plan for your videos and how it will support your SMART goals.

Before we get too far into the strategies and tips, if you need to know how to set up your own YouTube account, visit http://www.SocialMisAlignments.com/resource to get a complete video tutorial on how to set up your account.

Create your contact information and branded profile with CTA. YouTube recently modified their profile art specifications - included below are the latest sizes as well as the "safe area" that your text and logo will always be shown no matter how viewers are accessing your channel. Use keywords (SEO) in descriptions and include contact information and live links to your website and other social media sites in your description.

Advanced Note: Upload Channel photos 2560 x 1440 under 2 mg, note areas for various devices are: Desktop Max 2560 x 423, tablet 1855 x 423, desktop and mobile 1546 x 423 and the text /logo safe area for all devices is 1546 x 423.

Set up your marketing plan and agenda and make sure it coincides with your SMART goals for your practice.

With YouTube, just like other social websites, you will acquire your own audience. On YouTube, they are called subscribers. As with the other social websites, you will use a similar strategy to invite your patients and friends to subscribe to your YouTube Channel. You will also want to find channels that your ideal target audience subscribes to and comment on various videos. You may want to feature channels that your ideal target audience subscribes to directly on your channel to add to your credibility.

Unlike Facebook, on YouTube viewers are able to give a thumbs up (like) or thumbs down (dislike) on all videos. Or course you want a lot of thumbs up and it's even better if you can get lots of positive comments. All comments are public so you will need to monitor your videos even if you only upload videos once a week. Your subscribers, just like with other social network sites, will post questions and comments that need timely responses.

Maximizing YouTube for Your Practice

Most business owners make the mistake of simply uploading a video to YouTube. Some will go the extra mile and give it a catchy title and maybe a funny description. Sometimes their videos will go viral even when they do not pay attention to tags and keywords. They go viral because of their content, the relevance to their target audience and the fan base sharing it.

Prior to uploading the video, you will need to decide the type of video you want to create. There are eight different types of videos:

1. Talking head – where you talk directly to the camera.
2. Demo – you demonstrate your product or service benefits.
3. Process – give patients an overview of your services.
4. Screen capture- you share information from your computer.
5. Dramatic – enacting something.
6. Humorous – entertain and make people laugh.
7. Location – show patients how to find your practice and what it looks like inside.
8. Introduction – introduce yourself, your practice and your staff.

What are People Videotaping?

You can videotape just about anything you can imagine! Remember videos need to follow the same content guidelines as with other media websites - follow your 80/20 rule. Videos should not all be promoting and "selling stuff." You are sharing a story in your videos. They need to have a purpose and that is why they need to be pre-planned.

Videos should be a specific promotional campaign that demonstrates how to use a product or how a type of treatment is performed. For example, imagine that your massage therapist took a continuing education class for massage cupping. You promote it as a new service with photos and descriptions but patients are not booking the service. Now you get a friend to be your model for a video and you briefly demonstrate (1-2 minutes) what massage cupping is and how it can benefit patients.

Next, you make a second short video (1-2 minutes) with your friend describing how they felt after the treatment. Then upload both videos onto YouTube with an offer to try the service and your contact information. Lastly, post the links to the videos on all your other social media network sites. Do you think anyone would want to book an appointment once they saw how it works and heard how good it felt?

You can also use one video to answer a common question that many of your potential patients have. You can upload that video to your FAQ page on your website, post a link on your social media sites, include the link or embed it in your e-newsletters or embed it into your blog. You have a variety of ways to utilize the video.

Do I Need Expensive Equipment to Make a Video?

The short answer is no, you do not need expensive equipment to make a video. (That is not to say that if you plan to sell DVD's of your services or create a CE Course, then you would need specialized equipment and lighting). Most digital cameras have good video capture on them, the newer smart phones and tablets have quality video or you can purchase a good video camera for about $100 or less. Included below is a 10-point checklist for making a video.

Lighting – make sure your face is in good lighting; most treatment
    rooms have low lighting, for good reason. However, if you are

shooting a demonstration video, you want people to be able to see it so the lights need to be much brighter.

Rehearsal Run-throughs – Shoot the video or a shorter version of the video then review it to make certain there is proper lighting, the sound is good and there are no background noises.

Be aware of your surroundings – standing in front of a plant might sound good, however, on camera does it look like it is growing out of your head? Also, be sure your clothing color is not blending into the background.

Imagine the camera is a person and you are having a conversation with just one person. Speak directly to the camera and be sure to use "you" and do not use broad terms like, "to all my patients," "everyone," "they" or "him and her."

Just Breathe – many times people get a little nervous on camera.

Speak at an Even Pace – some people, when they get nervous, will start out slowly then speed up as they keep talking, while others will talk fast. The opposite is true as well, do not speak too slowly – keep an even pace.

- Scripting – make a "script" of highlights of what you are going to say, however do not rehearse it so much that you sound like a robot on the video. Definitely plan what you want to say so you aren't rambling and know ahead of time what action you want the viewer to do next. Some examples of action steps would be:

- Ask them to go to your website.
- Subscribe to your blog.
- "Like" the video.
- Leave a comment about the video.
- Make a purchase.

Just be sure at the end of each video you include for the viewer what their next steps are.

Adding a few Visual Effects – introductory music (make sure its royalty free), fading in and out, or a clickable link to website or other social media are good items to add. You do not want to "overuse" effects, but adding a couple of effects gives the video a professional look.

Consistently Upload Videos – you want to be consistent. As with other social media sites, you need to effectively utilize YouTube. This means you do not want to upload 10 one day and nothing else for several weeks. It is better to upload one every other day when you first start and then once a week is sufficient.

Keep Videos Short – in order to have the best results, keep your videos to 1 to 2 minutes. If you are demonstrating a product or treatment that requires longer time, consider making them into a series of videos. Even though 1 minute does not sound like a long time, you would be surprised how much information you can share in 60 seconds.

There are common mistakes in making videos that everyone has made, including me. On the next page are some of the items you will want to avoid.

Keep your YouTube videos separate from the rest of your marketing – integrate, integrate, integrate! Cross promote and add videos into all your marketing.

Forget to add keywords (SEO) and tags to videos – people forget this valuable step all the time or choose keywords which have nothing to do with their campaign.

Using a fake voice – you want to connect with your audience, so, use your normal speaking voice. Some people get really nervous on camera and try to over compensate by being "extra bubbly."

Seeming unfriendly – people will sometimes become nervous on camera and lose their energy. (This "puts viewers to sleep.") Speak with a smile but do not force it. (Try adding a mirror at the back of the room or next to the camera during rehearsal so you are aware of your facial expressions.) Remember, this is supposed to be fun!

Not talking to the camera - if you are using a tablet or laptop, the camera is usually located in the top of the screen. Many will look directly at the screen and will miss making eye contact with the viewers. Treat the camera lens as if it was your favorite patient and the two of you are having a casual conversation.

Trying for the perfect take – believe it or not, people like to connect with "real" people. If your presentation is too perfect, it sounds phony or canned. Not that you want a video with a bunch of mistakes, however a slight pause, stutter or laugh, is okay.

Extra noise – exclude as much background noises as possible - this means turn off phones, radio and TV. Put the pets and children in another room. Avoid being next to appliances (even microwaves and some refrigerators make a low humming sound that you do not realize is coming through on the video tape.) Avoid tapping of keys on keyboard and close the windows to eliminate outside noise, too (trains, traffic and airplanes all produce white noise that can be distracting for your viewers). Some people think that having a CD with calming music playing in the background is the same as adding music to a video - NOT! This only distracts the viewer. Add your royalty free music in later; YouTube has a music selection that you can match to the video topic.

Leaving the description blank – too many times people forget to add a description. Be sure to include a live link and ways to connect with you. Include your phone, email and website information and make it a live link. To add a live link to your website, instead of typing SRBSolutions.net you will add http://www.srbsolutions.net or sometimes just adding the www in front will make it live.

One hit wonder – do not just make one or two videos and never post again. As previously mentioned, videos are one of the most popular items for social media, so be consistent. Schedule your videotaping so you constantly have something new to upload.

Never using video at all – you do not need a healthy budget, expensive equipment or soundtracks. Plan your content (testimonials, demonstrations, introductions, and more… you have a VARIETY of options).

Advanced Note: When adding keywords (SEO), remember to add them to the description, title and tags as long as it is relevant to what is happening in the video! Too many times people will add keywords that have nothing to do with the topic of the video, this does not help you, in fact, and it could hurt you.

10 Action Steps for YouTube

1. Create your YouTube Channel and review how to set up videos.
2. Create professional graphics for your channel, remembering the text and logo are to be in the text/safe area for all devices.
3. Craft your video marketing plan and agenda, making sure it fits your SMART goals.
4. Write outline/script for your videos and review the video checklist.
5. Be consistent - continue to make videos and upload them regularly.
6. Add relevant keywords and tags to your videos.
7. Include CTA's, contact information and live links in your descriptions.
8. Have fun and speak directly to the camera - speak as if you are having a conversation with your favorite patient.

9. Invite your patients to subscribe to your channel.
10. Feature channels that your ideal patients subscribe to.

As mentioned previously, videos are one of the most popular items online. More than 60% of people prefer to watch a video over reading text. Look for ways you can incorporate videos into all areas of your marketing, including your website. Almost every website has an "about us" section. Consider creating a video containing this information. The video can contain the exact same information that is in the text. By offering another avenue for people to get to know you, you are appealing to a larger group of people.

Have fun with it, be creative... lights, camera, ACTION!

Need more YouTube tips? Be sure to download the outline for creating the perfect video on our www.SocialMisAlignments.com/resources page.

Chapter 11
"Pinning" Strategies for Pinterest

All puns aside, welcome to the hottest and largest virtual bulletin board of its time! Pinterest is the latest craze to hit social media and it is growing exponentially every month. Unless you have been locked in a treatment room for several months, you have probably heard about Pinterest. But you might be wondering what all the "fuss" is about, right? Well, you have reached the right chapter; take a photo tour of Pinterest, evaluate why your ideal patients are spending so much time on it and how you can adapt it as a social media source for your practice. According to Pinterest, millions of people use it daily to explore their interests, find products and services to buy and connect with people who share common interests.

Pinterest, like other social media sites, offers business accounts. Unlike others, you do not have to have a personal profile to have a business account. Hurray! Business accounts are a recent addition to Pinterest and you can easily change your personal account to a business account by clicking on your profile in the upper right corner and selecting settings from the drop down list. From there, you will be prompted to change your account to a business account. Select a business type and you are now a business account. Super simple! Included is a photo of where to find this on Pinterest.

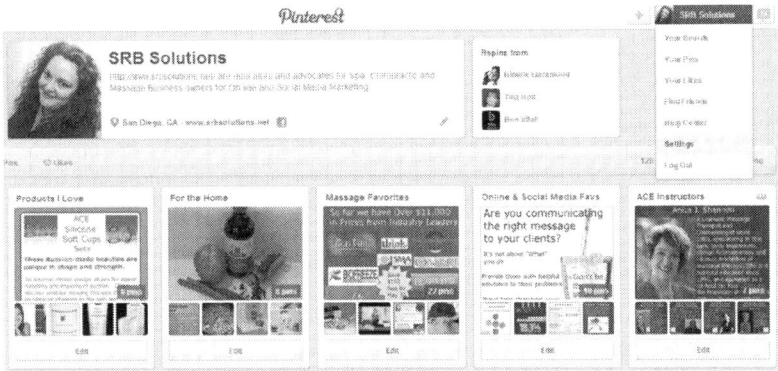

Be sure to edit your description with CTA and keywords (SEO) and a live link to your website or other social media links.

Create an eye catching profile photo size of 160 x 165 pixels. This is a small area so you may want to upload a quality photo of yourself, to work in that "personal" aspect or upload your business logo. Some people like to upload photos of pets, flowers or other "cute" objects as their profile photo. This is not recommended because it does not have a clear representation of you or your company. A better strategy would be to upload a text photo such as a CTA or special offer. (See the examples below of some profiles with logos and CTAs.)

Advanced Note: Add a pin it button to your website so your audience can pin your content from all possible locations, or add links to your other social networking sites in your description if you do not have a website.

How Pinterest Works

A pin is an image or video that people add to Pinterest. The pin it button captures images from the web and displays them on this virtual bulletin board called "boards". The "Pin it" button is another great reason you use high quality (professional) images that are royalty free or ones you have purchased. The easier you make it for your audience to pin from your website the better chance you have of getting discovered on Pinterest. Another great benefit: The "Pin it" button automatically inserts a link directly to your webpage.

Advanced Note: Use rich pins to automatically include information like prices, availability, ingredients and reviews with your pins and add meta tags to your website – register at business.pinterst.com for more details. Rich pins currently are only used for products, recipes or movies.

A board is a group of pins (images) that are the same theme. For example: "Nothin' but the Facts" – facts about ACE Massage Cupping as seen in the next photo.

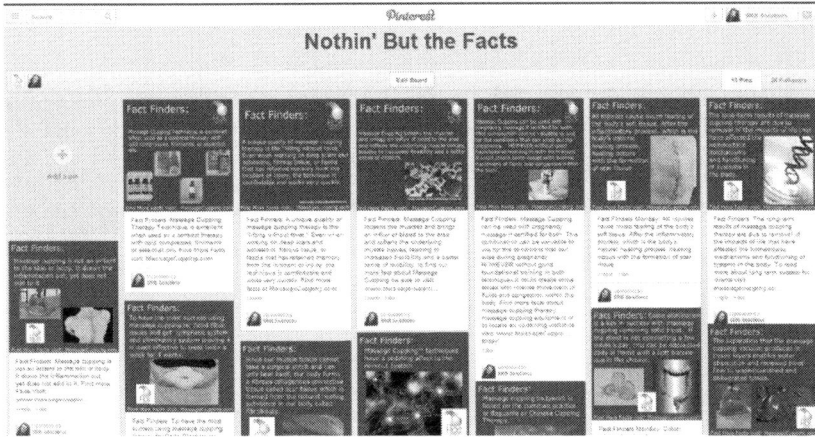

Consider how you organize your boards and pins based on interests of your ideal audience. Create a variety of boards that showcase your personality and highlight the benefits your care gives your patients. Each board has a cover pin that can be changed. Create a cover pin for each board that best captures the purpose of that board visually.

Advanced Note: Start a board of customer reviews (testimonials) that include both written reviews and videos.

Create curiosity and intrigue by using the "secret boards" for special offers or prelaunch new services that are only available for customers that buy from you. Give it a fun theme and make it a benefit so others will want to join.

Similar to finding other Facebook pages, you will want to find other boards that your ideal patients are following. And follow, re-pin and comment on them. Incidentally, there is more to come about the power of re-pinning a little later.

You can create an unlimited amount of boards and themes and each board can have a limitless number of pins.

Advanced Note: Use keywords (SEO) in the titles of your boards and pins and add CTA live links to websites or contact information in the descriptions of the boards.

The goal is to have a lot of followers that are re-pinning, following and commenting on as many boards and pins as you can. A good strategy for local chiropractors is to highlight your most-pinned products or services on your website. Below is a small sampling of the hundreds of people who have pinned images from our SRB Solutions website.

The most repeated image is the "FREE REPORT" image. This is especially important because that pin button from the SRB website shares the link for people to register by entering their name, email and mobile phone to receive a FREE report. By adding the "Pin it"

button to the website, we have created an automated way to increase our email list.

The second most popular pin from the SRB Solutions website is a link directly to one of our services, our SRB Authentic Evaluator. This service allows customers to book an hour for us to have a marketing and strategy conversation about their practice. These pins generate approximately five new customer calls per week from people interested in booking their strategy session.

Special note: The bulk of the SRB Solutions pins have been liked and re-pinned by their friends. This is like getting hundreds of referrals!

Imagine if you implemented a similar strategy for your chiropractic practice! What offer do you think your ideal patients would like to receive and pin? Are you beginning to see how powerful a social media site Pinterest can be?

Advanced Note: Add the Pinterest icon to all online and offline marketing (emails, newsletter, postcards, business cards, fliers, website and ads).

Who Uses Pinterest?

Thanks to the direct connection with both Twitter and Facebook, the user base continues to explode and females are the majority. Is your primary ideal audience married females, ages 35 to 55? If so, Pinterest should strongly be considered as your next social media website! More males are joining the ranks, so do not rule this option out entirely if your ideal patient is twenty something men. Pinterest has broadened their user fans by creating apps for Facebook, iPhones, tablets, websites and mobile websites in an effort to entice a larger demographic to join.

Best Types of Images

You are able to pin a multitude of images including photographs, infographics, videos, diagrams, cartoons and illustrations.

Use professional artwork and make sure it is royalty free or photos you have purchased and have permission to use. Include text around the images that shares helpful information, tells a story or shows how to make something.

Ideas for Content

When creating ideas for content, use your SMART goals and keywords and ask yourself, "where does my ideal patient fit?" Use a variety of different types of images for your pins. Think like your ideal patient when you are creating pins for your boards. Maybe one of your boards can be healthy recipes. Boards that are really hot right now are gluten-free recipes. Stay within your scope of practice when sharing content. If you are trained or certified as a nutritionist or dietician, be aware of the implication of your content when you pin. If you are a certified aromatherapist or have had training with essential oils, maybe one of your boards could be recipes to make special essential oil blends, aroma bath salts or special tinctures. If you are not trained, you can still create and maintain these boards; just be aware of the implied message and how you are positioning yourself when you share the information.

Create a board for each of the other services you might offer such as nutritional counseling or weight loss plans. Have boards that feature your retail products or re-pin your favorite product pins. **Hint: Most of the chiropractic manufacturers have Pinterest accounts and have created wonderful images of the retail products you sell. So, rather than creating your own pin, you can just re-pin retail product pins from your favorite manufacturers. Be sure to include your contact information or website link when you re-pin**.

Because you want to use the 80/20 rule, create one board that is personal. Ideas for what could be pinned on this board might include:

- Vacation photos and recommendations of things customers can do when they visit the vacation site.
- Staff videos sharing their bios.
- Personal insights from you and your staff about why you chose to become a chiropractor.

Create a Group Board and invite your patients to contribute. Invite them to post pictures of their pets, their favorite recipe or where they like to travel.

Create a board of inspirational quotes, sayings or favorite books. Invite patients to contribute or use this as way to generate a contest.

One important item that you want to do is to add website links or contact information along with a CTA and description to every Pin! Really pay attention to this part. You will have 500 characters to describe your pin, so be sure to include the basics such as relevant keywords (SEO) in your description. Add a live link to your website and ask a question for them to re-pin, like or make comments to.

Speaking of re-pins, remember the chapter about Twitter and re-tweets? A similar philosophy applies to re-pins. The majority of your pins should be new pins by you. Use re-pins of the boards your ideal patients are following periodically or the influencers for your ideal patients. Ultimately, you want people re-pinning your content. It is even better when an influencer from the profession re-pins your content. Do not take the lazy route and let others do the pinning for you. It is okay to show you are "in the know" by re-pinning relevant information. Just ensure the majority of your content is new pins that you created.

How Often to Pin?

Your boards should look full; how often you pin will depend on the number of boards you create. Pinterest recommends pinning once a day. If that feels excessive, then commit to three pins a week to start. A board has five pins highlighted: the main pin and four spaces that show below it. When you create a new board, try to have five pins so all those spaces are filled. I've included a photo on the next page. Notice the featured pin is large and 4 smaller photos underneath would be blank if I didn't have at least 5 pins to the board.

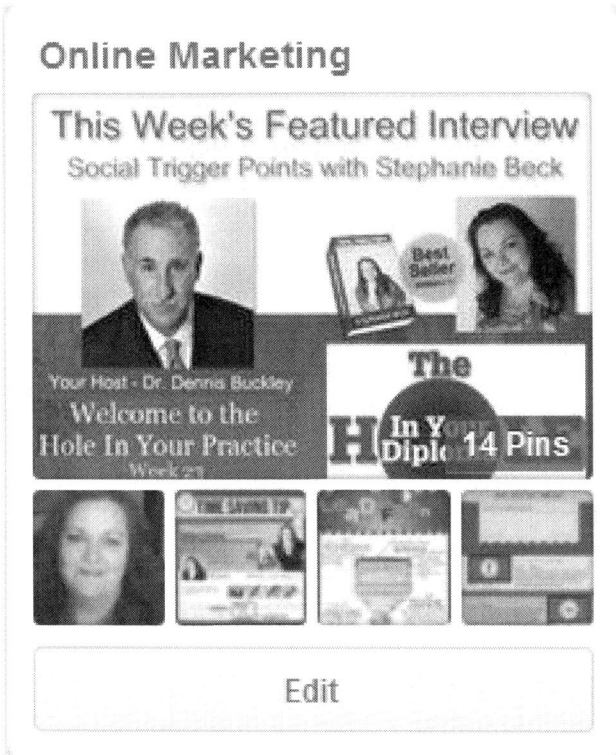

Are you starting to see how Pinterest can be a powerful social media website for your chiropractic practice? To recap, your action steps are included below.

10 Action Steps for Pinterest

1. Create a business account or change your personal account to a business account.
2. Add CTAs, keywords (SEO) and live links to your website in your profile description.
3. Use a professional photo, logo or CTA for your profile.
4. Add the **Pin it** button and set up your website for Rich Pins.

5. Create a content agenda and measure against your SMART goals and plan your strategy.
6. Add CTAs, relevant keywords and contact information to your pin descriptions.
7. Be strategic with your re-pins.
8. Ask patients to follow your boards and re-pin your information.
9. Be creative and consistent when pinning.
10. Create images on your website to encourage more pins and automated list-building opportunities.

Are you inspired? Do you have a better understanding of the power of pinning? It is important is to keep your SMART goals in mind so that the boards and connections you are making are going to provide the results you want.

For those who like to do-it-yourself, I have included a few graphic sites that help you build info-graphics for Pinterest on our www.SocialMisAlignments.com/resource page.

Chapter 12
LinkedIn Connectors

You have your marketing plan and you have set up your Facebook, Google+ and Pinterest business pages. You are tweeting and videotaping and perhaps tweeting about videotaping, but have you thought about LinkedIn for your practice?

As reported by LinkedIn, there are 225 million total users and two new users join every second. The most interesting change made recently was the addition of Company Pages. To date, there are two million business pages created since they became available in 2012. Why is this important to your practice? Unlike other business pages, LinkedIn company pages are a lot like having a mini-website, thereby offering some unique benefits that other social media websites cannot.

The Benefits of LinkedIn

Setting up a LinkedIn profile and company page for your practice provides a variety of benefits. If you invest a little knowledge and care, you should be able to reap the following four benefits:

1. Increase SEO results and in most cases, raise your brand awareness to within the top five positions in Google search results.

2. Add another lead-generating component to building prospective patient lists.
3. Geo-target patients connect with peers and locate the resources you need.
4. Increase your professional credibility.

Historically, B2B (business-to-business) companies gain quicker results on LinkedIn than B2C (business-to-consumer) however, both types improve lead generation and extend their marketing reach by implementing LinkedIn's unique features.

Begin by updating or creating your profile account. Included below are steps to maximize your impact.

1. Always use a professional photo – some people use a logo or CTA for this profile photo, since this is where you will be connecting with peers as well as customers. It is best to use a professional headshot. (Save the CTA and logo photos for your Company Page.)

2. Always use your name and only your name for your profile account.

3. Craft a catchy headline and be sure to use keywords (SEO) so you can be found on Google and within LinkedIn searches. You may also want to include an offer or free give away. I have included a photo to demonstrate where the headline is.

4. Start connecting with others - your goal should be to connect with at least 501 ideal patients.

5. Customize your website listing with free offers or CTAs - do this by selecting the "edit contact info," and then click on the pencil next to websites as indicated in the next two photos.

Next, select "other" from the drop down screen. This allows you to customize the different websites, blogs or other social media custom apps that you want to highlight.

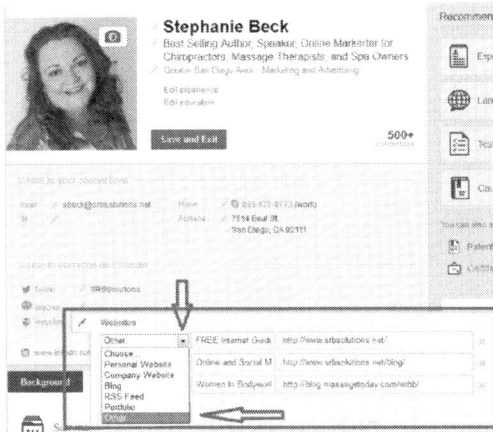

6. Complete ALL necessary contact information (email, phone, address, website and Twitter).

7. Keyword (SEO) your present and past work history.

8. Use keywords (SEO) throughout your summary and profile.

9. Use terms that your ideal patients will connect with when you are summarizing.

10. Add an offer and a CTA to the "Summary."

11. Use the "Projects" section to promote free downloads, showcase services and other special offers that your ideal

patients would like to have and include special offers for service or product from your company page.

Keyword your skills and expertise section with relevant terms your ideal patients want or need to the company page.

12. Add keywords to your experience section.

13. Make it a goal to get at least 10 recommendations (best way to get them is to give them).

14. The ultimate goal is to find and join 50 groups that your ideal patients are members in.

15. Include any media attention, honors and awards.

16. Set your Profile to "Public."

Advanced Note: Create a custom URL for your personal profile and include a keyword that your ideal patients will be searching for on LinkedIn.

The key to creating LinkedIn into a social media tool for your practice is having a powerful and professional presence. Similar to your other media websites, the goal is to strategically craft your profile with your ideal patient in mind before you begin connecting. Build your LinkedIn strategy so it supports and meets the SMART goals for your practice.

How Do Company Pages Help My Practice?

Now that you have upgraded your personal profile, concentrate on creating your Company Page. LinkedIn company pages are as valuable as Facebook or even Google+ pages. The reason is LinkedIn Company pages allow you to promote a variety of products and services with live links, video links and special promotional links!

Checklist of items you *must* have completed to create a LinkedIn Company page include:

- Your profile must be more than 50% complete to start a Company Page.
- You must have 30+ connections to start a page.
- Only current employees can appear on a company page.
- You must have a company email address. Gmail, Hotmail, and Yahoo emails are not considered company emails. (e.g. sbeck@srbsolutions.net is accepted srbsolutions@gmail.com is NOT accepted)

How to Create a Company Page

When you are ready, select "companies" from the menu tab, and select "add a company." You will be prompted to enter your company name and email address and continue through the process until you have all the information completed. Lastly, select the "publish" button.

Once you have published your page, you will be able to add on other items. For example, you can post a job under the "careers" tab.

One of the most important sections under the "admin tools" tab is the "add a product or service" area. From this section you will be able to add the following for each product or service:

- Direct links to your website.
- Custom graphics.
- Features and benefits (remember to use keywords your ideal patients will use).
- Upload a link of a YouTube video about the product or service.
- Create a special offer and link to a promotion.

Invite your patients and connections to follow your page and create a marketing plan for your company status updates. Coordinate these updates with all other social website updates. Include a variety of types of posts and use the 80/20 rule. Just like other social network sites, consistent company updates keep you at the top of the LinkedIn and Google search results. Current, valuable and relevant information keeps your connections engaged and interested and it's how to stay active.

Also, make a note to check your "Page Insights" tab frequently. This tab will be your best friend for providing a comprehensive overview of your company as well as page visitor demographics.

Participating in LinkedIn Groups to Grow Your Practice

The next benefit of LinkedIn that you need to know is Groups. These are slightly different from the Google+ community and Facebook groups. Remember, more than 85% of users on LinkedIn are professional, therefore the groups and their discussions are usually of a problem-solving nature: people asking advice or seeking recommendations for products and services. You can find the same types of groups on Google+ community pages or Facebook groups, but the tone and voice are generally not the same as on the LinkedIn Groups. Be sure to review group rules and guidelines and search for groups where your ideal patients belong.

Your role in the group is to be helpful - participate by asking questions and providing solutions. Rarely do you find a group that allows direct promotion. However, when you actively participate and provide valuable information, you will find those ideal patients visiting your company page and profile. By engaging weekly with your targeted groups and discussions, you can gain new patients.

One crucial part that can dramatically increase the number of new patients is having both the profile and company page completed with live links to lead capture offers. These can be on your website or a custom app on other social media sites such as Facebook. Each lead is sent a series of emails with more helpful tips and information tailored for the ideal target patients.

Advanced Note: Add the LinkedIn "Follow" button for your Company Page to your website.

If you are still on the fence whether LinkedIn can be a valuable business website or not, consider this recent stat – it is estimated that more than 45% of consumers will search LinkedIn for professional services. Because LinkedIn has the reputation of being "the social media site for professionals," does it not make sense for you to have a professional presence on this site?

14 Action Steps for LinkedIn

1. Create your Personal Profile – add CTAs, keywords or offers to your headline.
2. Use a professional photo and company email.
3. Add keywords throughout your profile and include a link to your Company Page.
4. Get at least 30 connections and 10 recommendations the first week – ask and give recommendations regularly.
5. Always send a personal message with a connection invite.
6. Customize your website links with CTAs and special offers.
7. Craft your content agenda with your SMART goals in mind so you will achieve your results.
8. Create your Company Page.

9. Join and participate in Groups with your ideal patients frequently.
10. Send invites to follow your company page regularly.
11. Like, comment, share and create status updates for your company page daily – like and share your company updates from your personal profile.
12. Use a variety of media types for your content (photos, videos, links from other social network sites, articles and blog posts).
13. Check your page insights regularly to review your follower demographics.
14. Add LinkedIn to all online and offline marketing.

LinkedIn is more than just another social network. In January 2012, a HubSpot Blog reported that LinkedIn had the highest visitor-to-lead conversion rate at 2.74%, almost three times higher than both Twitter (.69%) and Facebook (.77%). So, why not use LinkedIn as a social media site for your chiropractic practice?

Follow SRB Solutions Company page to receive many more helpful tips you will find the link on www.SocialMisAlignments.com/profiles.

Stephanie Beck

Chapter 13
5 Common Mistakes and How to Avoid Them

E ver wondered what NOT to do on social media? I'm not referring to the legal and ethical guidelines associated with chiropractic care. I'm referring to the same mistakes 90% of chiropractors, organizations and business owners make when implementing social media strategies expecting to get new customers. Let's call these social misalignments– the social subluxations that need a little adjustment to create great communications, remove the blockages and build healthy relationships so you can have MORE new patients.

What to Avoid

The five most common mistakes chiropractors make in social marketing are:

1. Planning to fail.
2. Providing incomplete information.
3. Thinking social media equals instant patients.
4. Engaging in inconsistent and irrelevant sharing.
5. Seldom checking the tracking tools.

Do not worry if one or more of these mistakes are ones you might be currently making. There are many moving parts to managing a practice and the most important part to focus on is that you are now aware of it and are taking the steps to correct it.

Planning to Fail

You know the saying, "when you fail to plan, you plan to fail?" As with any type of growth for your practice, in order to have the best results, you need to have a clearly developed plan of action. When it comes to social media, chiropractors (and other healthcare practitioners) look past the value of planning. There are two ways I have seen this mistake.

Two Most Common Mistakes Made During the Planning Process

The first most common mistake happens when social media is not integrated into the general marketing plan. I have seen chiropractors invest thousands of dollars into websites, adword campaigns, search engine optimization (SEO) services, content for blogs, email campaigns, newspaper ads, radio spots and direct mail pieces and when I ask what they are doing on social media I hear - "Oh, yeah, we have social media, the office receptionist takes care of that." Social marketing is a powerful way to enhance all of your online or offline marketing. If you think your patients aren't using social media, here are some stats you may not be aware of:

> More than one billion users are logging onto Facebook monthly.

> More than 170 million people use Google+ daily.

> More than 400 million tweets are sent a day on Twitter.

> More than six billion hours of video are watched each month on YouTube.

Millions of married females age 35-55 use Pinterest daily.

More than 225 million users are on LinkedIn and two new users join every second.

In just a quick 10 minute search on Facebook alone, I found more than 300 groups with anywhere from 20 to1,100 people in them who share back pain and back related injuries and are looking for advice, recommendations and needing education on how to deal with it. But, you're right, why on earth would you want this FREE access to thousands of people when you can spend thousands of dollars on traditional marketing? Please forgive me; I am being sarcastic to prove my point.

Now, I will go on record here and say, I do NOT want you to STOP what you are doing with traditional online and offline marketing! Especially if it is bringing in new patients, by all means continue doing what you are doing.

What I want to make you aware of, if you weren't already, is the sheer volume of people that are already using social media daily and these numbers are continuing to grow exponentially.

The second most common mistake made during the planning process happens when a scattered approach is applied to posting. Once you have your planning strategies, go the extra mile to create a social media agenda for the week, month or year. There is nothing worse than the panicked feeling for yourself or your office manager when it's 2pm and you remember you haven't posted anything! Worse yet, you are scrambling to try to come up with something to post! When there is an overall strategy and a theme or plan for each day of the week or month, this gives some focus and should decrease the amount of time spent online because you are more efficient.

What to Consider Planning

Consider harnessing the power of social marketing to boost your return on investment (ROI) for the traditional marketing you are already doing. Keeping it separate is not an option. You should be incorporating it into the rest of your campaign. It can significantly increase your reach when done effectively.

Find out on which of the social media sites your ideal patients are spending their time on. That doesn't mean you have to be the one researching, although I do encourage you to spend some time (1 to2 hours) on the recommended sites yourself so you are familiar with them.

This is your practice and my guess is you would never intentionally give someone else full control of your reputation and your practice without having a plan of action, right? But if you are not taking an active role in your current social marketing that is exactly what you are doing. Social marketing can assist in building your practice, your reputation and relationships to prospective patients without you investing hours daily.

One of the best types of planning strategies is to follow the SMART goals format. (Remember, SMART goals are: Specific, Measurable, Achievable, Realistic and Time-bound goals). Next, you will want to identify your ideal patient. Finally, determine what you want to achieve through social marketing. Do you want to get reviews? Do you want to connect with your current patients? Do you want to build a list of new potential patients? All of these are possible with social marketing. Once you have set your SMART goals, work on your postings.

Incomplete Information

Another common mistake made is providing incomplete information. Once you have your SMART goals and have selected your social media sites, the next item that is commonly overlooked is making sure all the profile areas are completed. Because people trust social media sites more so than branded websites, they will generally use the social media sites to search for legitimate practices and information. In fact, YouTube, with more than one billion users visiting each month, is commonly referred to as the second largest search engine (Google of course, being #1) So if you are missing any valuable key points in your profile, you might be missing lots of opportunities.

What to Consider Completing

It never hurts to double-check. So be sure your basic information has been added to your social pages. Things like website, phone number, address, hours of operation and email address. Although about 90% generally have those, what typically get missed are the detailed items. Roughly 50% fail to include the mission statement, owner and staff bios and listing of besting selling products or services. Mostly missing are the live links to other websites, blog, newsletter, or special offers - only about 25% catch this part.

Here is another "biggie" that often gets overlooked. If you are using Adwords or SEO services or have a primary keyword you are paying to be ranked on page one of Google, then add that primary keyword into your profile information. You do need to phrase it so it flows naturally, much like you do on your website pages and in your blog posts. Less than 2% of the social sites I review have completed this part and yet it can be one of the most powerful items about social media marketing. This is important because social media references are showing up in search results when practices have listed relevant, legitimate keywords in their profiles and postings. In cases like YouTube and Google+ where information is indexed quickly (because Google owns those), when keywords are used correctly, some practices are able to dominate a page for a particular set of keywords by using them strategically with their social marketing.

Thinking Social Media Equals Instant Patients

The third most common mistake made is thinking social marketing will instantly produce new patients. Remember, first and foremost, these are "social" sites. To appreciate the advantage of social marketing, start by understanding the reasons why your patients and potential patients are using them. I understand your marketing goals for your practice might be simplified into three words: Branding, Selling and Promoting. However, when it comes to using social marketing, your approach is completely different. Most patients would categorize their time on social sites in one of the following:

- Wanting or needing to connect with other people.
- Needing emotional support, validation or recognition.
- Fulfill their need to have fun or for entertainment.
- A convenient way to get reviews on products and services from other people.
- A way to organize their personal or social life.

Patients are on social sites to visit, catch up on events, be educated, have fun and laugh, express their opinions and share their lives, hopes, dreams, hobbies and interests. One thing they are absolutely NOT using social sites for is to hear marketing pitches.

The good news is they WILL make appointments and buy your products but only if they are looking for wellness treatments in the first place or if the information you are providing through your social marketing interests them.

What to Consider

People like doing business with people they know, like and trust. Social marketing is one of the quickest ways to build this type of relationship. Therefore, start by thinking of social marketing as a way to build a "know-like-trust" relationship with potential patients. In order for your social marketing to work effectively, provide information that interests them but never pushes them. They will become patients if they are actively searching for your services or if the information you are providing interests them.

To create content that interests them, you will need to understand your ideal patients and what makes them tick. Concentrate on connecting and engaging with your ideal patient. They will always become the most active and engaged audience. These Ideal patients are the ones who will share the most, like your posts and answer your questions. You will start to recognize their social networking habits and what topics, words and emotions trigger them to take action. Then, it becomes much easier to craft the perfect posts that demand engagement.

Inconsistent or Irrelevant Sharing

The fourth most common mistake in social marketing chiropractors make is being inconsistent or irrelevant when it comes to sharing on their social media pages. Too many times when I am reviewing social media sites, I see there are time gaps between shared information. One of the benefits social marketing provides is the opportunity for your "voice" to go viral. Always acknowledge someone when they like, share or comment in a timely fashion. The other part of the mistake is when doctors share irrelevant content. Too many times they want to share what <u>they</u> want to be discussing instead of what their ideal patients and potential patients want to know.

Consider Sharing

Offering helpful information and links to sites that you find beneficial for your patients should be one of your top priorities. By offering them more information that helps them, you will begin to position your practice as their expert or "go to" person for advice.

Use professional graphics when at all possible. If budgets are limited then consider at least hire a graphic professional to create your timeline header and profile photos for all your social marketing. As you gain momentum, pay attention to where your patients invest their time. Are they spending time out of loneliness or isolation? Do they love to contribute to a cause? Understanding your Ideal patient's reason for using social media sites will help you supply the content they find more enjoyable. This will help to create a feeling of belonging or exclusive membership or private club with your target audience.

How Often to Share

This isn't a "set it and forget it" product: you or your office manager needs to check your accounts daily if possible.   Remember, one of the main reasons that people use social media sites is for validation, support and recognition, so reward them for contributing, sharing, commenting and liking.

Since you can capture a much shorter attention span, it is extremely important to be interactive and immediate when it comes to social marketing. Immediacy is a key component to keeping your audience engaged. Equate it to making a phone call to your friend, asking how they're doing and then hanging up before they can answer. Of course you wouldn't ever do something like that to a friend or a patient. But, that is what it seems like when you share information and they comment but there is no response from you for two or three days.   Keep a steady stream of information to avoid constricting your success by posting often and being consistent.

This isn't to say you need to spend hours on social media to have success. In fact, with some time spent in the planning stage, a good rule of thumb is to plan on 10 minutes three times a day (or a total of 30 minutes) to achieve SMART results. The reason "daily" is important is because of perceived expectation of people who are using social media sites. According to a recent survey by Oracle, one in six consumers on Facebook expect a response to their questions in fewer than 30 minutes - all the more reason to check your social media pages more than once a day. Another good idea is to make a habit of checking your social sites with the same frequency you check emails or voicemails.

There is an old saying in marketing that says "content is king" but when it comes to social marketing, engagement is what counts.

Engagement will vary depending on which social media sites you choose to use. For example, on Facebook your engagement is in the form of likes, shares and comments while on Google+ it is +1 and shares. LinkedIn engagement is in the form of likes, comments, follows and shares while on Twitter you can have replies, re-tweets, favorites, respond via emails and embedded tweets. Pinterest engagement is measured by pins, re-pins, likes, follows and shares while YouTube engagement is measured by likes, dislikes, comments, favorites and features.

Engagement is so valuable because the more engagement you have on your page, the higher you rank in the newsfeeds of your audience. It isn't just enough to have them like or follow your social pages. They need to be interacting with your updates on a regular basis. If your ideal patient and potential patient are not engaging with your updates regularly, the social sites see that patient as one who does not value your content. Therefore, your posts will not rank as high on their newsfeed when they are using the site, or even worse, the site will stop sharing your feeds with that patient all together. That is why consistent and relevant content that your Ideal patients value and respond to is crucial to building your "know-like-trust" relationships.

The average person only spends 20 minutes a day on social media sites. The readers will generally respond and interact with the pages that are highest in their newsfeeds. If you are only posting once a day or you skip two or three days, your posts will most likely be buried by other pages and friends who want to connect with them and have posted content consistently. If you are not interacting with your ideal patients by asking questions, sharing content that is relevant to what they are looking for, or providing them with offers to do business with you, chances are your ideal patients will not ever see your posts.

Speaking of offers to do business with you, as I said before, social media is NOT a place for you to constantly be promoting your practice. However, it is a great place to offer ways to connect with you off social sites. What I mean by this is to have one offer a week for your ideal patients and potential patients to join your mailing list in exchange for something of value to them. This could mean a free set of videos, a report, a 20-minute health consultation, a free spinal check or some other type of offer. As you build rapport with your ideal patients, you will be earning the right to ask for their business. So, while I don't want you to be pitching your practice all the time, if you are posting informational type content consistently, then you should give the patients the opportunity to connect with you at least once a week. I like to use the 80/20 rule for content, 80% of the time make the content informational and 20% of the time make it promotional.

Because this is a social site and we know people like doing business with other people, the 80/20 rule applies here as well. Eighty percent of your posts should be health and wellness related, while 20% of the time it should be personal. It's okay to show vacation photos, inspiring quotes, ask about weekend plans, or share hobbies because that makes a connection with your ideal patients. They see you as a real person. So when you are creating your social media agenda, include some personal items as well. Almost always, the personal updates will have much more engagement than your practice updates. The most important part is to be strategic with the updates. If you know personal updates guarantee you more engagement, and then schedule the offer 2 to24 hours after those types of updates. You want to post your offers when your engagement is the highest so you will reach the greatest of number of your ideal patients.

So, be strategic with your offers, specials, contests and other promotional items and place them when you engagement is at its peak. To help you remember how valuable engagement is, I personally like what international social media expert Mari Smith says about engagement on social media: "content may be king, but engagement is queen and she rules the house!"

Never Checking the Tracking Tools

The fifth and final common mistake I most often see with chiropractors is failing to utilize the tracking tools on social media sites. All social media sites offer different types of tracking tools and even some like Facebook have enhanced their tracking tools. They will tell you what days of the week your fans are spending time on Facebook, as well as the best time of day to post. Most sites offer reports that can be downloaded to review your updates and see which ones were most viewed by your fans. This is extremely valuable information and confirmation that you are achieving your SMART goals. One of the benefits of using SMART goals is the results are measurable and time based. Therefore, in order to know you are achieving your SMART goals, you need to be able to track how you are doing. Remember, it isn't about who has the highest number of potential patients on a page, it is about the quality of the ideal patient. I would much rather have 500 ideal patients that are inspired, interested and taking action, than to have 1500 fans that never participate.

Since most of social marketing is relationship building, engagement is crucial to measuring success. Each of these social media sites has insight tools that provide a variety of data and stats. There is value in analyzing updates; you can split-test different types of offers at various times of the month to see which ones have the most engagement.

I am also continuously surprised at the number of chiropractors who do not know how much traffic they are getting to their website. I recommend you add some metrics to your website so you can track the amount of traffic you are getting from your social marketing. Google analytics is a free service that can be attached to most sites. If you use a template on a shared server, check with your provider to find out what kind of analytics they offer.

What to Consider Analyzing

What you need to be analyzing is the how many of your followers are talking about you from your reports and whether the general number of followers are increasing or decreasing. Also pay attention to the number hides, unlikes, spams, unfollows, unsubscribes or dislikes on your social sites. If you start to see a drop in your engagements, first analyze what has changed. Did you share too much information on a particular day? Did you post too many offers? Did you change update times and did you respond to all questions and comments? Sometimes it can be holidays or certain times of the year that the level of activity on social media sites will vary. If you have a cold winter climate, you may see a slight rise in activity because people are not able to be out and desire more interaction. Summer can sometimes be challenging because people are busy and not updating as often as during other months. This is why you need to monitor weekly or monthly and plan your offers, campaigns and special promotions to boost engagement during the lulls or run them when your engagement is at its peak.

Another item to analyze is your type of updates. The various types of updates are:

- Links to videos
- Photos
- Links to your website
- Links to blog posts
- Infographics
- Uploaded videos directly to the social site
- Text updates
- Fill in the blank
- Links from other sites (like article or directory sites)

Keep content fresh by using different types of content in your updates. In general, photos and videos will always be more popular than direct links and text updates. You may find that photos get more likes but videos get more shares and status updates get more comments. That is why you need to analyze more than just the general engagement on the page; you need to also look at what kind of updates received the highest amount of engagement.

Stephanie Beck

Summary
Ready…Set…Take Action!

A s mentioned at the beginning, whether you love it, feel it is a waste of time, or just do not understand it, the important fact is what your customers think about social networking. Hopefully, after reading and implementing action steps throughout this book, the term "Social Media" has a friendlier face for you, or at least you can understand how it can benefit your practice.

Some common themes you may have noticed throughout are:

- Plan with Specific, Measurable, Achievable, Realistic and Time bound (SMART) goals – start with an end in mind – everything you do has a purpose
- Be strategic with your time, content and planning
- Always be consistent with your messaging, voice and your brand – never "set it and forget it"
- Remember to have fun and apply the 80/20 rule
- Understand how your ideal patient is using a particular social media and adapt your message to connect with them
- Build know-like-trust relationships
- Your purpose is NOT to sell products or services

With the rapid rise in popularity; social networking sites are not going away any time soon. That is why knowing the psychological reasons patients use social media and how that can affect your practice is so important. Apply the strategies provided so you can maximize your time and presence. The biggest reason why most business owners fail is that they never take action. You have an opportunity, if applied properly, to use these top six social media websites to skyrocket your chiropractic practice.

Let's get connected! I will follow, fan, subscribe, connect, like, share and comment on your success! Comment on Facebook or one of your favorite social networks by letting me know how much you enjoyed this book. All links to my social media sites are available at: www.SocialMisAlignments.com/profiles.

About Stephanie

Stephanie Beck is a passionate educator and advocate for the online marketing success of small businesses. After more than 15 years in the health and wellness profession, Stephanie started SRB Solutions to focus on helping small businesses navigate through the new world of social and online marketing.

She is a Bestselling Author of, Small Business Trendsetters Volume 2 and Social Trigger Points. Stephanie has served as a published guest columnist since 2003 with several magazines including: *Dynamic Chiropractic Practice Insights*, *Massage Today*, *Massage Magazine*, *Practitioner Magazine* and *Marketing Matters*.

She also is a contributor for the Women In Bodywork Business blog. Known for her social media and marketing experience, Stephanie contributed the chapter on Ethics in social media for The Ethics of Touch 2nd edition by Dr. Ben Benjamin & Cherie Sohnen-Moe.

Stephanie and her team are very active on social networks. SRB Solutions was awarded the Kudzu Best of 2012 Online & Social Media Marketing in San Diego. More than 5 million businesses competed across 30 categories, and winners were awarded based on the highest number of votes received on Kudzu.com.

In 2013, the overall results of a new Internet-based post by which locals were asked to name "Social Media Expert of 2013" produced well known marketing and advertising consultant Stephanie Beck more than any other name in San Diego.

Stephanie was quoted in over 230 business journals, radio and television stations including CNNiReport, the Wall Street Journal Market Watch, the Atlanta Business Chronicle, Los Angeles Business, the Washington Business Journal, KFMB TV News Center8, the Boston Business Journal and more. Stephanie has a Bachelor's Degree in marketing from University of Central Missouri, has served on the ISPA Education Committee and Editorial Advisory Board for Massage Magazine. In 2012 she earned her Local Marketing Consultant Certificate through Marketing Mastery Association.

She was elected to the Alliance for Massage Therapy Education Board of Directors in 2012 where she currently serves as Website and Marketing Director for the non-profit education organization.

Connect with Stephanie on Social Media, leave a comment on Facebook or one of your favorite social websites and let her know how much you enjoyed this book and she will be sure to follow, fan, subscribe, connect, like, share, comment and retweet your pages as well!
Have questions? Be sure to send an email to:
www.SRBSolutions.net.

Made in the USA
Charleston, SC
12 June 2015